SAN FRANCISCO PENINSULA BIRDWATCHING

Sequoia Audubon Society, San Mateo County, California

with members of the
Golden Gate Audubon Society,
Metropolitan San Francisco

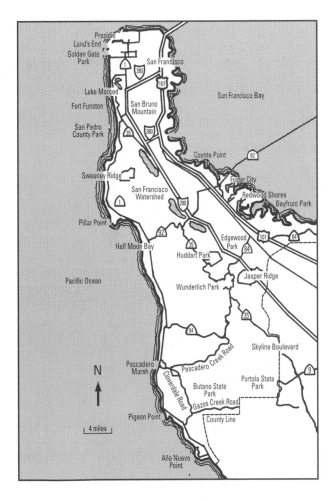

Dedicated to all those who have stepped where they
shouldn't while looking up for that one rare bird.

Editor: Cliff Richer
Cover illustrations: Dan Keller
Illustrations: Dan Keller, Terryl Graves, and Mary Molteni
Maps: Wayne Benson, Nancy Conzett, Sharon Hom, Donna Kirsacko and Cliff Richer
Word Processing: Lisa Moody, Janet Murphy, Francis Toldi and many of the authors.
Design and Composition: Fog Press
Design and Production Assistance: Harriette Judge
Printing: IPC Communication Services

Publication Committee: Francis Toldi, Chairman; Mary Bresler, Debbie Frantz, Harriette Judge, Dan Keller, Rich Kuehn, Peter J. Metropulos, Cliff Richer, and Dean Schuler.

Contributors: Sequoia Audubon Society: Jean and Frank Allen, Rick Baird, Wanda Belland, Mary Bressler, Nick Coiro, Al DeMartini, Sharon Hom, Rick Johnson, Dan Keller, Donna Kirsacko, Peter J. Metropulos, Carol Miller, Donna L. Peterson, Cliff Richer, Wilma Rockman, Robin Smith, Scott Smithson, Judy Spitler, Tom Taber and Francis Toldi, Golden Gate Audubon Society: Alan Hopkins, John "Mac" MacCormick, Dan Murphy and Mary Louise Rosegay

Published by Sequoia Audubon Society, 30 West 39th Avenue, Suite 202, San Mateo, CA 94403

Copies may be ordered from the publisher.

Library of Congress Catalog Card Number: 96-69663

San Francisco Peninsula Birdwatching, revised edition

ISBN 0-9614301-1-7

1 2 3 4 5—99 98 97 96

The descriptions of Golden Gate Park, The Presidio, Lake Merced and Lands End originally appeared in *The Gull,* the newsletter of the Golden Gate Audubon Society, as did any maps by Nancy Conzett.

CONTENTS

❖

PREFACE

❖

The San Francisco Peninsula is blessed with a magnificient avifauna and with many accomplished and articulate birders. This book combines the best of both, with detailed descriptions of and directions to the best locations for birds in our region written by a group of our most outstanding local birders. This is a substantial revision of the title by the same name published by Sequoia Audubon Society in 1985.

Production of this volume was a team effort. All chapters were written by members of the Sequoia and Golden Gate Audubon Societies. Sequoia members edited, field-tested, transcribed and proof-read all the copy. All of those who contributed to this project and to the previous volume are acknowledged on the title page. We give them our heartfelt thanks; without their hard work this book would not have been possible.

On a personal note, without diminution of my appreciation of all who participated on this project, I would particularly like to express my thanks to Cliff Richer for his sensitive, yet sure, editing of the diverse manuscripts submitted by the contributors, to Jim Beley at Fog Press for his patience and essential technical advice; to Peter Metropulos for keeping a careful eye on the ornithological accuracy of the book as a whole (not to mention his authorship of several excellent chapters); to Dan Keller for his superb illustrations; to Barry Sauppe, for his willingness to share his extensive knowledge of birds in general and San Mateo County birds in particular; and to the other members of the Book Revision Committee for many hours of behind-the-scenes work.

Thanks again to all, and happy birding!

Francis Toldi
Chairman, Book Revision Committee

INTRODUCTION

❖

If you are either a tourist who looks only for cable cars and famous bridges or a businessman or businesswoman who is visiting the electronic workshops of Silicon Valley, you may think of the San Francisco Peninsula as being thoroughly urbanized with a birdlife consisting of House Sparrows, Rock Doves and European Starlings.

On the other hand, if you're a follower of Christmas Count results you may see that our three Christmas Counts are extraordinarily high, with the Crystal Springs and Año Nuevo Counts consistently ranking in the nation's top 10 and with the San Francisco Count surpassing that of any other all-urban area year after year. Your vision of the San Francisco Peninsula may then be of one vast aviary.

The truth lies somewhere between. Bounded on three sides by the Pacific Ocean and San Francisco Bay, the Peninsula contains an astounding variety of habitat in a compact area. The deep off-shore waters of the Pacific are in binocular range at Pigeon Point where Black-footed Albatross, Sabine's Gulls, a variety of shearwaters and alcids and even a Mottled Petrel have been seen from shore. The shallow waters of the bay have attracted Black Skimmers from the south and, for three winters, a Smew from the north. Golden Gate Park in San Francisco, as well as Moss Beach, Princeton Harbor, and Gazos Creek along the coast have become famous for vagrant passerines. Open fields and hillsides, dense redwood forests, coastal scrub, salt and freshwater marshes, ponds and streams, dunes and beaches, mudflats and tidal pools are all present here—each with its own avian population. Eight, perhaps nine, species of owls breed on the Peninsula. Every season brings surprises—Yellow-billed Loons, Tufted Ducks, Sharp-tailed, Buff-breasted and Stilt Sandpipers, Northern Parulas, a Rustic Bunting. Over 400 species of birds have been recorded from the area—and all are available with no more than a 90 minute drive. Birds, like people, find it a great place to visit and to live.

If ever there was a labor of love this book is it!

All of us who participated in this project, in both editions, are enthusiastic birders of varying skill. Some of us are novices who typed near-illegible handwritten manuscripts and faithfully followed sometimes vague directions so that you wouldn't have to. Others, like Barry Sauppe, Dan Keller and Peter Metropulos—"industrial strength" birders who can hold their own with the best in the world—lent their birding expertise. We are attorneys, teachers, gardeners, business owners, managers, executives, clerks, cooks, students and retirees. Some of us are in our teens; others in our seventies. We have little in common other than our interest in birds and in sharing "our" birds with you.

Wherever it was practical, we asked the first-edition authors to review and update their chapters. When this wasn't possible we sought out people who were most familiar with the areas to do the revision. Most of the chapters needed extensive revision or even a complete rewrite. This is not a criticism of the earlier authors but reflects the changes that man and nature have imposed and are imposing on the environment. As we go to press many of the areas are changing. For example, hydrologists and biologists are initiating changes to restore Pescadero Marsh to its original condition and each year greater numbers of elephant seals, once believed extinct, crowd the beaches of Año Nuevo Point. Unfortunately most of the changes are neither so well-intentioned or so wondrous. Development threatens more and more of our scarcest habitat. This book owes its existence to the work of countless thousands of environmentally conscious private citizens who have worked and continue to work to preserve our natural heritage. With their help we hope to keep issuing new and expanded revisions of this guide.

Anne Scanlan-Rohrer, editor of the first edition, did a superb job and we will be happy if this edition turns out as well. Nevertheless, we feel you'll find improvement in two areas.

In 1985 deadline considerations caused Anne to use a number of less than high quality illustrations. (I can be critical without offending anyone in this respect since it was my sketchbook that Anne co-opted for most of the illustrations.) Although you will find a very few of these drawings included for continuity, most have been replaced by superior artwork.

The organization of the book has also been changed slightly. We have included San Mateo County's San Bruno Mountain in with San Francisco as it is aligned geographically more to Lake Merced and Fort Funston than to the Peninsula's other birding spots. South of Daly City the guide follows the Peninsula's three north-south transportation corridors. Highway 101 and the Caltrans commuter railroad parallel the bay shore; Highway One follows the coast; while Interstate 280 and Skyline Boulevard run down the spine of the Peninsula. Whether you're traveling by auto or by public transportation, we think you'll find our orientation along these three routes to be logical and easy to follow.

We hope you enjoy the book as much as we enjoyed doing it.

Cliff Richer
Editor

GUIDELINES, ADVICE, AND GENERAL COMMENTS

❖

- Respect private property. Most farmers don't mind if you walk around the edges of unposted and unfenced fields, but don't do this in fields of flowers or ready-to-harvest crops. These have been subjected to depredation in recent years and you may end up having to explain your presence to a sheriff's deputy. If there is any doubt don't enter private property without permission.

- Learn to recognize Poison Oak and avoid it!

- Coastal cliffs are often undercut by erosion. Obey all signs and avoid cliff edges unless you're absolutely sure they are solid.

- As of this writing Lyme disease is not a problem in coastal California, but we do have ticks, so take normal precautions.

- Our local rattlesnakes are rare, timid and not terribly poisonous. Nevertheless, why take a chance that "your" rattlesnake may be the exception? If you should encounter one, leave it alone.

- A spotting scope is desirable for all coastal or bayshore birding. A zoom lens can be valuable in scanning for off-shore birds.

- You'll find a San Mateo County checklist in the appendix. Field copies may be obtained from Sequoia Audubon Society, 30 West 39th Avenue, San Mateo, CA 94403. Call 415-345-3724 for prices. Checklists are also available for Foster City and Pescadero Marsh. The County Parks also have checklists.

- While we have included some minimal information on public transportation, we have avoided specifics. We found that this information changes so often that detailed bus routes or train schedules can be erroneous, misleading and counter-productive. Instead we have listed the local transportation agencies in our "References and Resources" section.

- Weather and climate, particularly along the coast, are changeable and surprisingly cool year-round. Dressing in layers under a lightweight windbreaker is recommended in any season. Beware of sunny days as well. A bright, but cool and windy day along the coast can produce a magnificent burn!

- Be careful if you walk on our rocky shores. The rescue of some unfortunate fisherman or rock-hopper stranded by high tide is a regular occurrence.

"Rogue" waves are common and can cause anything from a dunking to severe injury and worse. The Coast Guard and some local fire departments have units that specialize in the recovery of drowning victims. Don't let them practice on you!

- The maps are intended to show you where to locate the birding sites, but are not meant to be trail guides. For detailed information on particular trails we recommend that you consult Russmore and Spangle, *Peninsula Trails.*

- Plant names used in this text follow Hickman, *The Jepson Manual.*

- Each birding area has an informal rating by season, ranging from four stars (outstanding birding) to one star (of moderate interest).

SAN FRANCISCO AND SAN BRUNO MOUNTAIN

Dan Keller

Anna's Hummingbird

GOLDEN GATE PARK

❖

Dan Murphy

Spring ★★★
Summer ★★½
Fall ★★★
Winter ★★★★

San Francisco's Golden Gate Park is among the finest urban parks in the world. It is wholly man made except for land forms and isolated oak groves in the eastern part of the park. The park is dominated by a forest of exotic trees, primarily Monterey Pine, Monterey Cypress, Blue Gum (eucalyptus) and small numbers of a wide variety of other trees. The forest is broken by many fields and over a dozen small lakes. The park functions as a habitat island, and the avifauna is abundant in terms of both species and overall numbers.

The western part of the park offers the richest birding opportunities. Weekdays and weekend mornings are certainly the preferred times to visit this area. Holiday and weekend afternoons are so heavily impacted by people that birding is poor in all parts of the park. Kennedy Drive and the area around the concourse and museums are closed to automobile traffic on Sundays and holidays. Middle Drive is closed on Saturdays. There is an effort being made by some skaters and bikers to extend the closure. Isolated areas in the eastern part of the park are best avoided when birding alone.

Bird populations vary extremely between and during seasons. Spring begins in mid-February with the migration of Allen's Hummingbirds and Tree Swallows. From mid-March until mid-May is the best time to look for nesting species. Spring migration peaks during March and April. Summer months are slow, but birds which breed locally remain in the area through August. Fall migration begins in August. Eastern vagrants begin to arrive in early September and continue to pass through until mid-October. Migrants and vagrants continue to be present in small numbers through the winter. By November the wintering population begins to peak. The San Francisco Christmas Bird Count, usually scheduled for a weekday between Christmas and New Year's, generally turns up a number of unexpected birds in the park.

The Eastern Developed Area

Stanyan Street West to Crossover Drive

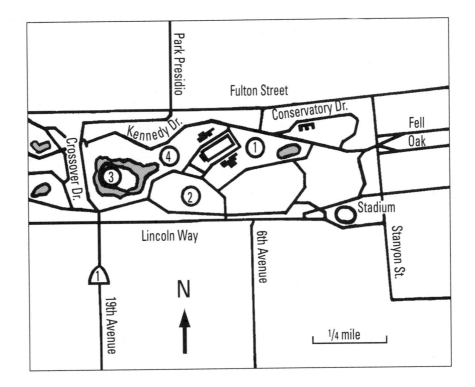

Much of the eastern part of Golden Gate Park is no longer worth birding. Many of the plants in the Fuchsia Dell have matured, died and have not been replaced, so that area seems to be less used by hummingbirds than in the past. The oaks along the northeastern corridor of the park do not form a fully functional ecosystem and are not as attractive to birds as are natural oak woodlands with their understory of shrubs, wildflowers, grasses, mosses and lichens. A small, perhaps irregular, population of Western Screech-Owls does inhabit the oak woodlands. Both the oaks and the fuchsia areas are isolated and may not be safe for single birders.

The **Rhododendron Dell** (#1), located east of the Academy of Sciences and south of Kennedy Drive at about Sixth Avenue, is an area with enough habitat value to be attractive to birds, particularly in spring. The hill in the middle usually has a resident pair of Rufous-sided Towhees. The trees in the area may provide roosting sites for Band-tailed Pigeons. This is an irruptive species however, and the pigeons may not be present every year. Watch for Red-shouldered Hawks, Scrub Jays, various flycatchers, Orange-crowned, Townsend's and Wilson's Warblers, Fox, Song, Golden-crowned and White-crowned Sparrows.

Strybing Arboretum (#2) is by far the most diverse plant community in the park. The botanical exhibit is excellent and the birding is good. Be sure to check one of the maps posted near each entrance. A bird list may be available at the book shop by the main entrance gate. Birding is best in winter and spring. Bird numbers drop in summer, but residents can be found. The area has not been well covered during the fall, but common residents and migrants are certainly present, and vagrants can be expected among feeding warbler flocks.

Among the wintering rarities noted recently have been Red-naped and Yellow-bellied Sapsuckers, White-throated Sparrows, Summer Tanagers, and a variety of vagrant warblers. The pond near the Eugene Friend Gate, across the street from the Japanese Tea Garden, is packed with gulls and ducks during fall and winter. Green-winged Teal, Ring-necked Ducks and Buffleheads can be found during most winters. Gulls may include Mew, California, Glaucous-winged, and Western.

For land birds take the path west (right) from the Eugene Friend Gate for about 50 yards to the fork. Watch for a wintering sparrow flock which usually includes White-crowned, Golden-crowned, Fox and Song Sparrows as well as an occasional White-throated Sparrow or two. At the fork take the path around the left side of the Eastern New Zealand plant bed. Check the trees at the end of the bed to the right and those to the left along the edge of the meadow for sapsuckers. Red-breasted Sapsuckers are regular here in winter and both Red-naped and Yellow-bellied Sapsuckers have been found several times. Continue along the paved path past the meadow, to the Japanese moon viewing garden, then continue along the path to the left (watch for Varied Thrushes) back to the South Africa area. This, the Eastern New Zealand and the adjacent Cape Provinces Exhibits offer the richest birding habitat in the arboretum. Look through the trees and shrubs for roaming flocks of insect-eating birds. These fall and winter flocks often include vagrant warblers. The arboretum harbors what may be San Francisco's last flock of California Quail. Once common throughout San Francisco's parklands, this bird has nearly been extirpated by the feral cats that roam the city. The arboretum offers many other interesting plant communities. California native species (great for butterflies), redwood forest, dwarf conifers and the succulent garden are but a few of the exhibits. The latter can be excellent for hummingbirds. Blooming eucalyptus trees in the area attract warblers, including the occasional American Redstart. A paved path going east from the Eugene Friend Gate can be productive too. If nothing else the flowers will attract your attention. Rhododendrons are seldom out of bloom here.

Stow Lake (#3) is the most widely used lake in the park. The walk around it is about three quarters of a mile. The island in the middle, Strawberry Hill, is accessible by two bridges. A dirt path circles it and winds its way to the top. A small snack bar and boat rental facility are located at the northwest corner of the lake. Restrooms may be found behind the building.

Check the area around the concession for gulls and ducks. Ring-necked Ducks may be seen here in winter. A large flock of Brewer's Blackbirds inhabits the small island near this area. This same island is the only Great Blue Heron nesting site in San Francisco. Look for this heronry on the west side of the island. From the concession walk east until the road straightens out. Check the eucalyptus trees across the street for flycatchers, warblers or sparrows. Western Tanagers can be found here during spring and fall migrations. As you continue around the lake be sure to check the islands for Black-crowned Night-Herons. At the point where the road turns to the right and follows the contour of the lake take the path to the left. This goes down to the Japanese Tea Garden. If today's birding is good in the eucalyptus trees check this path and the oaks at the bottom of the hill.

Ducks expected on the lake include Mallards, American Wigeons, Ruddy Ducks, Lesser Scaup, Ring-necked Ducks and Buffleheads. Migrating Green-winged and Cinnamon Teal may be on the lake between late January and April. Wintering gulls will include Mew, California, Western, Glaucous-winged and perhaps Ring-billed. The city's first record of Tufted Duck is from here.

Strawberry Hill, the main island, can be very productive in fall. During September and October it usually provides habitat for two large flocks of insectivores. These flocks are dominated by Yellow Warblers during the early season, and Yellow-rumped Warblers by October. Check the flocks thoroughly for vagrants. Though ignored by most local birders, this could be among the park's richest vagrant traps.

Adjacent to Stow Lake is the **Pioneer Log Cabin** (#4), situated on the edge of a meadow with a nice picnic area and excellent birding habitat. Not only do the trees here change with the seasons, but the variations in light, wind, and fog conditions make this among the most visually attractive locations in the park. A rich variety of migrant and resident birds use this area. Watch for Western Tanager, Wilson's, Orange-crowned, Yellow and Townsend's Warblers, Pacific-slope Flycatchers and Cedar Waxwings. Many vagrants have been recorded here as well. Among them are Tennessee Warblers, Blackpoll Warblers, Bay-breasted Warblers, a Hooded Warbler and American Redstarts. The place to look is the hillside behind the log cabin. The vegetation there includes eucalyptus, hawthorn, blackberry, German Ivy and a tangled mass of other shrubs and vines.

The Western Undeveloped Area

Crossover Drive West to the Great Highway

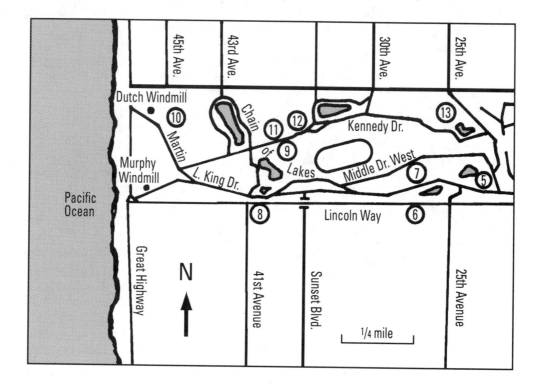

West of Crossover Drive the park is less developed than the eastern half. The woods here provide a windbreak for the more formal planting to the east. It lends itself more to leisurely walks and more gratifying birding experiences.

The area north of Lincoln Way between Crossover Drive and Sunset Boulevard can provide excellent birding. The eucalyptus, pine, and cypress woods open to several meadows and three lovely lakes. Here you can find areas of solitude and unique beauty. To bird the area adequately plan on walking around each lake, going off the beaten path into meadows and through the woods, and following bridle paths instead of the streets.

Elk Glen Lake (#5) is a good place to start. Located at the foot of the 25th Avenue entrance and Martin Luther King Drive, the lake has been a valuable duck habitat in the past. Its value declined during the recent drought, perhaps because the lake's water supply was frequently interrupted and the lake was sometimes reduced to little more than a puddle. Ring-necks, Ruddies, American Wigeons, Mallards and Buffleheads can be expected here. Watch for a Belted Kingfisher which flies between here and other lakes in the area. A Red-breasted Sapsucker often winters near the fruit tree on the north shore of the lake. Look for warbler flocks in the eucalyptus just north of the lake. A sparrow and finch flock usually winters in the weed patch at the lake's east end. At dusk a Great Horned Owl sometimes flies over the lake.

Return to King Drive and go right to **Mallard Lake** (#6), about a quarter mile west on the south side of the street. There are more secluded paths in the woods on both sides of the street. Mallard Lake is a great duck feeding pond for those with a loaf of old bread. Even in summer there are a few Mallards around. But from September through April the flock includes not only Mallards, but American Wigeons, Ring-necked Ducks, Ruddy Ducks, Buffleheads and an occasional Eurasian Wigeon. Watch for Green-winged and Cinnamon Teal, Gadwalls, Northern Shovelers, and Common Goldeneyes. All of the expected gulls use the lake but Mew Gulls seem to particularly enjoy this pond. Land birds occur in small numbers too. Black Phoebes, Downy Woodpeckers, Chestnut-backed Chickadees, Brown Creepers, Pygmy Nuthatches, and Song Sparrows are only a few of the possibilities. A Great Blue Heron and a Great Egret can usually be found at this or the other lakes in the vicinity. Green Herons and Black-crowned Night-Herons are seen less frequently.

Check the meadow across the street for birds perching in the trees around its edge. Band-tailed Pigeons are a possibility as is the seldom seen Barn Owl.

From here continue west. If you are on foot, walk to the 30th Avenue entrance to the park. A path comes down the hill from the left and continues on the right. Follow it through the valley about 200 yards to Metson Lake. If you are driving, continue west, turn right at the first street, then turn right again. Continue to the top of the hill to Metson Lake. Note that this road, Middle Drive, is closed to automobile traffic on Saturdays.

During recent years **Metson Lake** (#7) has lost much of its attraction to birds. Wood Ducks no longer appear regularly in the park, presumably because of breeding habitat loss elsewhere in their range. California Quail are no longer present, most probably because of the number of cats and unleashed dogs in the park. Mallards and wigeons are the most common winter residents. They may be joined from time to time by other ducks, gulls and a heron or egret. Spring and summer bring out a few swallows. In winter the nearby woods are good for

Hermit and Varied Thrushes, while Pygmy Nuthatches, Downy Woodpeckers and California Towhees are here year-round.

To return to your starting point continue east along Middle Drive until it ends at Transverse Drive, turn right and turn right again at King Drive for the return to Elk Glen Lake. If you are on foot just turn right after you pass the fenced maintenance yard and continue straight ahead to Elk Glen Lake. To go west turn around and follow the road beyond the Polo Field, down the hill to its merger with King Drive at the southeast end of the Chain-of-Lakes. If you are on foot take any of the trails in the area. One goes west from the south end of the lake. During the spring Red-shouldered Hawks and Olive-sided Flycatchers can be heard calling in this area. This can be an interesting area for nesting species, particularly in shrubs west of the forested area.

Chain-of-Lakes (#8,9,10) transects the park between 41st Avenue and Lincoln Way and 43rd Avenue and Fulton Street. These three lakes provide one of the best and most popular birding sites in the park. Varied habitats appear to be the key to the value of this area. Well-intended but poorly-planned maintenance projects have been mixed blessings for these lovely little lakes. South and Middle Lakes are in generally good condition, although some of the most valuable habitat was "cleaned up". North Lake has lost much of its habitat value. Efforts to seal the lake's bottom failed and the northern third of the lake is diked off and dry during much of the year. That area is devoid of shoreline vegetation. The other two-thirds of the lake is well vegetated, but frequent changes in water level have caused it to lose much of the avian diversity it once supported.

To bird this area begin at the parking lot between South and Middle Lakes. From here it is an easy walk to any of the other lakes. If the lot is full park on Kennedy Drive near its intersection with Chain-of-Lakes Drive.

South Lake (#8) is good for ducks except in the summer months. It usually harbors a number of Mallards, American Wigeons and coots. A Great Egret can often be found along its shoreline. The shrubs and trees on the west side of the lake may hold Varied and Hermit Thrushes, Chestnut-backed Chickadees, and a variety of other small birds including occasional vagrants.

During fall migration or when the eucalyptus trees are in bloom this area may be temporary home to a few vagrant species.

Middle Lake (#9) is among the most productive and popular birding areas in Golden Gate Park. From the parking lot between South and Middle Lakes take the trail leading to the lake. Between September and April, sparrows abound in this shrub-dominated habitat. Look in the bushes to the right for a place where local residents feed some of the park's many feral cats. Unfortunately this is also a favorite spot for Golden-crowned and White-crowned Sparrows, California Towhees and Dark-eyed Juncos. California Quail, once abundant here, have been extirpated.

At the fork follow the trail to the left. Fall-flowering eucalyptus, combined with fruiting *Myoporum* and blackberry provide a food base for many migrants. Watch for warblers, particularly Orange-crowned, Yellow, Townsend's, Yellow-rumped and Wilson's. The insectivore flock which forms in August should also include Pacific-slope Flycatchers, Western Wood-Pewees, Olive-sided Fly-catchers, Bushtits, Ruby-crowned Kinglets, Warbling Vireos, Western Tanagers and, as the season progresses, a vagrant vireo or warbler. Don't discount the possibility of seeing migrants more common to the interior. Among these might be a Solitary Vireo, Common Yellowthroat, Yellow-breasted Chat, Black-headed Grosbeak or Northern Oriole. Many of the warblers of North America have been seen here or at North Lake at one time or another. Tennessee Warblers, Blackpolls and American Redstarts are among those seen almost every year. Expect to see just about any migrant North American passerine here. Continue along the path past the little meadow to the redwood grove. Check it thoroughly during migration. The least you will get are a few Orange-crowned, Yellow or Yellow-rumped Warblers. But like the nearby eucalyptus trees, this grove too holds a special attraction for vagrants, so expect almost anything.

Continue north and check the open water for ducks. Green-winged Teal, Northern Shovelers and Wood Ducks are likely to be among the flock of Mallards and wigeons. Pied-billed Grebes, Double-crested Cormorants and American Coots are usually present on the lake as well. Follow the trail right around the lake. Bird the insect-rich willow grove at the east end for insectivores, hummingbirds, finches and sparrows. Fall and winter vagrants to this niche have included a Yellow-green Vireo, Chestnut-sided Warblers, Tennessee Warblers and American Redstarts.

The stream which bisects the hill can be productive if it is running or if its pools of water have not yet dried-up. Despite its concrete bed this stream is a wonderful place to bird in spring. Flowering eucalyptus may attract migrant flycatchers and Western Tanagers. The mature woods host cavity-nesting Downy Woodpeckers, Tree Swallows, Pygmy Nuthatches and Brown Creepers. The forest canopy may harbor nesting Red-shouldered Hawks, Mourning Doves, Common Ravens, American Robins, California Towhees and Pine Siskins. Ground and shrub nesters may include Rufous-sided Towhees, Wilson's Warblers, Dark-eyed Juncos and White-crowned Sparrows.

Back at the lakeside trail, continue south. Check the oak just where the trail turns west for a Hutton's Vireo in spring. Song Sparrows can be found in the marsh all year, but fall migrants and winter residents make this an excellent spot for general birding. Vagrants are always a possibility. Western Wood-Pewees, Olive-sided Flycatchers and Pacific-slope Flycatchers usually spend time in this area between August and October. Western Tanagers are generally numerous and the occasional Black-headed Grosbeak may be joined by a Rose-breasted Grosbeak. Accipiters hunt this area between September and April and, though never common, they should be watched for.

North Lake (#10) is just to the north and west across Kennedy Drive. Redevelopment projects have not been kind to the environment of this pond. Its habitat value has crashed, due in large part to the removal of vegetation and lack of water . However Red-winged Blackbirds and Song Sparrows still nest in the marshes and, during fall and winter, Mallards inhabit the open water of this lake where they are often joined by Double-crested Cormorants, Pied-billed Grebes, American Coots and a variety of gulls. A Great Egret and a Great Blue Heron can usually be found along the shoreline.

Take the paved path around the lake to the right. Migrant warblers are most often found in shrubs and trees along the north end of the lake. A bridge at the southwest corner of the lake marks a spot to look for Northern Waterthrush provided the lake's depth is high enough to flood the stream bed west of the bridge. Just to the north check the island to the right for migrants in spring and fall. It has been an excellent site for birding in the past, and it can be expected to be so again once the lake's artificial habitat is stabilized. This southern part of the lake has produced virtually all western migrants expected along the coast as well as such rarities as a Philadelphia Vireo, Northern Parulas, and a Prothonotary Warbler. Other islands should be checked for roosting ducks and herons. This lake provides night sanctuary for several hundred ducks which roost there during the winter.

As the path turns to the right just past the little island with the swamp cypress, go left across the street onto a dirt road and check the woodlot which is bounded by the golf course to the south, the archery field to the west and Fulton Street to the north. This is one of the oldest pine stands in the park. It is dominated by the European Maritime Pine (*Pinus pinaster*). During nesting season look for all the common park cavity nesters. Fall and winter bring insectivores to the canopy and seed-eaters to the forest floor. At any season the actual birding can vary from exciting to dull. Exercise caution at the western end of the wood lot since arrows do occasionally find their way into the woods. Do not go inside the *Myoporum* hedge as this forms the barrier between the wood lot and the archery range.

Return to the lake by any of the trails and continue back to the starting point. If the northern end of the lake is stabilized and re-vegetated it may become a rich area for ducks and gulls once again. The east side of the lake does not usually provide the best birding. Despite this, be sure to check the willows on the island for chickadees, bushtits and warblers. Anna's and Allen's hummingbirds, Black Phoebes, Song Sparrows and White-crowned Sparrows can also be found in this area.

Other Golden Gate Park Sites

The Buffalo Paddock (#11), just east of Chain-of-Lakes Drive on Kennedy Drive, can be a wonderful birding spot. Don't count on infinite variety here, but instead regard it as an opportunity to observe avian behavior. A large blackbird flock utilizes this fenced meadow all year so you can observe interactions between the dominant Brewer's Blackbirds and the large numbers of Red-winged Blackbirds, Brown-headed Cowbirds and starlings. To the patient observer, much can be revealed by watching the group dynamics of the mixed flock. In the fall or winter, you may also find a Tricolored Blackbird. The meadow also hosts a large wintering population of Killdeer. Common Snipe winter here from time to time. Red-tailed Hawks have nested on the north side of the meadow and one or two usually winter here. Late summer and early fall bring a profusion of grass and weed seeds which attract large numbers of House Finches, Pine Siskins and a few American and Lesser Goldfinches.

 Spreckle's Lake (#12) is just east of the Buffalo Paddock. Developed for, and still used by model boat hobbyists, this is a favorite spot for all our wintering gulls. It is one of the park's best sites for seeing Western Grebes, Canvasbacks, Ruddy Ducks, Buffleheads, and Lesser Scaup. A visiting Greater Scaup is a real possibility and Tufted Ducks have turned up as well. Look overhead for all the park's swallows: Tree, Violet-green, Cliff, Barn and Rough-winged.

 Lloyd's Lake (#13), about a mile east of Spreckle's Lake and just west of Crossover Drive, is a nice spot to look for our more common ducks. It is a favorite spot for Ring-necked Ducks. You can usually find a Belted Kingfisher here as well. Be sure to check the north shoreline for waders, including Black-crowned Night-Herons and Green Herons. A walk to the area just north of the lake can be interesting. This once was the park dump and the variety of vegetation and its proximity to the lake provide good habitat for a number of species. Pacific-slope Flycatcher has been heard singing in this area during nesting season.

 Final Notes: There are a number of species that can be expected throughout the park. Red Crossbills are the first to come to mind. They can be present throughout the year and may be abundant in irruptive years. Listen and watch for them in any of the coniferous forest areas. Red-shouldered Hawks, Anna's Hummingbirds, Downy Woodpeckers, Pygmy Nuthatches, Brown Creepers, Bushtits and Chestnut-backed Chickadees are hard to miss if you spend an hour's birding almost anywhere in the park. Hawks such as Sharp-shinned, Cooper's and Red-tailed winter here. There are records for many other species as well. Cedar Waxwings seem to erupt in their April and May migration and can be found just about everywhere.

. . . And the Final Note: Remember that Golden Gate Park is a completely artificial environment. As such it is fragile and susceptible to incredibly rapid changes such as those witnessed at Chain-of-Lakes in recent years.

Dan Keller

Scrub jay

LANDS END

❖

Seal Rocks and Lincoln Park
Alan S. Hopkins

Spring ★★★
Summer ★
Fall ★★★★
Winter ★★

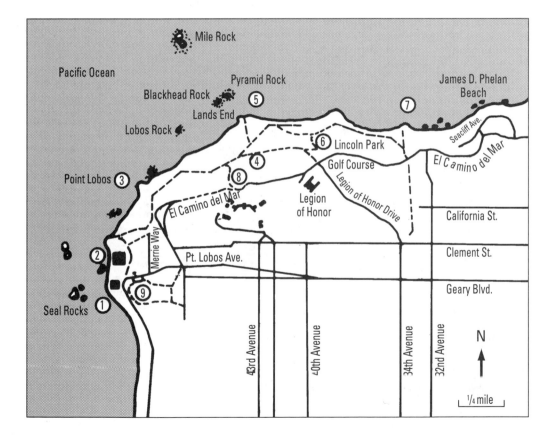

Lands End is an area of breathtaking vistas and dynamic bird life. The rocky cliffs and small beaches make it the best place to observe ocean and shorebirds in San Francisco. However, the most attractive aspect of Lands End is the observation of migrant land birds. On a good day it is possible to see migrant hawks, flycatchers, orioles, tanagers, sparrows, and warblers. During a few days each spring and fall, a "wave" of migrants will pass through and warblers can be seen by the hundreds. The best time to look for spring migrants is from mid-April to early June; the height of fall migration is from mid-August to mid-October.

The weather plays a key role in the presence of migratory birds along the coast. Knowing and understanding the weather can greatly increase your chances of seeing a wave of migrants. There is a constant struggle between the cold water and air from the Pacific Ocean and the warm inland temperatures. This struggle is manifested as wind and fog. On a day when the temperatures are in the 80's in Oakland or San Jose, it might only be in the 60's in San Francisco. The typical San Francisco weather from May to October is fog along the coast in the morning, lifting and burning off with the strong afternoon breezes. It is the presence of fog that brings and holds migrants to the coast. Fog patterns are quite variable. The best waves usually occur when the fog is low in the morning, and lifts in the afternoon but does not burn off. On warm days, with little wind and the fog sitting on the ground in the morning, burning back to the ocean or outer avenues, but not lifting, can be good too. Some of the most exciting birding can be from dawn until about 11:00 a.m. on the first few days of a heat wave. When the temperature starts to rise over the low 80's in San Francisco, the East Wash can be teeming with birds that feed at first light, but fly off before noon. On clear windy days, as far as migrants are concerned, you might as well sleep in.

It is possible to check all the best spots in the area by making a large loop of the trails and roads that follow the coast. A good place to start is the parking lot at Merrie Way above the Cliff House and Sutro Baths. As in most urban parks, it is a good idea have a friend along and to avoid leaving valuables in your car.

Depending on tides, you may decide to begin or finish birding at the **Cliff House** (#1). The birds are most easily seen here at high tide. The observation deck behind the restaurants is the best place to scan Seal Rocks, which abound with bird life. American Black Oystercatchers, Western Gulls and Brandt's Cormorants all nest on the rocks. In June the rocks are covered with Brown Pelicans and their cohorts, the Heermann's Gulls. In mid-July the shorebirds begin to reappear; look for Wandering Tattler, Willet, Surfbird, Ruddy and Black Turnstones and Sanderlings.

After the Cliff House, the next spot to check is the remains of **Sutro Baths** (#2). Just below the coffee shop is a trail that leads to the old baths. The baths are no longer used by swimmers, but are a favorite spot for gulls and shorebirds to drink and bathe. In the winter small numbers of waterfowl stop on the ponds. Mallards, American Wigeon, Ring-necked Duck, and shorebirds not associated with rocky shores such as Black-necked Stilt, Pectoral Sandpiper and Red and Red-necked Phalaropes are possible around the ponds. Tufted Ducks have been seen here with some regularity in winter.

The large flat cement area on **Point Lobos** (#3) to the north on the ponds is an excellent spot to scope for seabirds. In fall and winter the ocean becomes alive with Red-throated, Common, and Pacific Loons, Western Grebes and Surf, White-winged, and Black Scoters. A strong incoming tide produces a choppy rip line where the water from the sea and bay meet. It is along that choppy line where seabird watching is usually the best. Bonaparte's Gulls and Forster's, Caspian and Elegant Terns come to feed on the rich waters churned up in the rip. Some of the more pelagic birds possible are Parasitic and Pomarine Jaegers, Common Tern, Sooty Shearwater, Northern Fulmar, and Black-legged Kittiwake. Alcids such as Marbled Murrelet and Cassin's Auklet have been found. A sharp eye can usually find a Common Murre any month of the year. Mammals found here include California sea lions, harbor seals, and, with some luck, harbor porpoises during the Spring. California gray whales have passed within 100 yards of the point.

To continue the loop, take the steps up to the row of cypress trees at the end of the parking lot. Follow the last trail that heads northeast at the east end of these trees. Keep to the right until the trail meets a dirt road. The road is actually an old trolley car track bed that ran from downtown San Francisco to the Cliff House. The cliffs along the way can be good for seabird watching. In the summer there are usually a few Pigeon Guillemots on the large rock to the east.

From this point the trail goes slightly inland. After about a quarter of a mile there is a large grassy open area which is good for finches. This area is the bottom of the **West Wash** (#4). As the road bends to the north, watch for the paved road on the right. This road leads to the Palace of the Legion of Honor through Lincoln Park Golf Course. Head up the road only as far as the large willow patch. The willows are most productive when they bud in the spring, at which time they are swarming with Anna's, Allen's and some Rufous Hummingbirds; there may also be Hutton's Vireos and Purple Finches around. During migration this spot is worth checking for warblers and flycatchers. If you wish to skip this spot, the paved road is a shortcut to the East Wash.

To continue the loop, go back to the dirt road and watch for a trail on the left by some trash cans. This trail goes down to **Lands End** (#5). From the tip of the point there is a fine view of the coast. Scoping the water below Mile Rock has produced Marbled and Ancient Murrelets and is an especially good spot for loons. Closer to shore are Pyramid Rock and Blackhead Rock where Pelagic

Cormorants roost. In the winter of 1979 these rocks were frequented by two Harlequin Ducks. Although the willows and cypress behind the small beach look inviting, birding them is not advised.

Return to the main road and continue east. After a short distance watch for the new trail that goes up the hill on the right. This trail continues the walk, but in summer you may want to go past it to check the bottom of the sheer cliff for Pigeon Guillemots and harbor seals.

At the top of the new trail are trees that border the **East Wash** (#6). These trees are among the most productive for migrants and have produced rarities; Kentucky Warbler, among others, has been seen here. The East Wash is actually a landslide in progress. In the stormy winter of 1982 the whole area was moved three feet closer to the sea, and the old trail was destroyed in the process. To check the wash, take the trail that leads up the wash as the main trail bends back towards the coast. From the large flat area be sure to check the large fennel (anise) patch. All the trees and shrubs that surround the wash are worth checking since rare birds have been found in almost all of them. Some of the "goodies" that have been found include Hooded, Worm-eating, and Blackburnian Warblers, Indigo Buntings and Rose-breasted Grosbeaks along with some unusual western birds like Green-tailed Towhee and Common Poorwill.

To go to the next spot, backtrack to the main trail. As the trail rounds the point the foliage becomes thicker and there are usually Chestnut-backed Chickadees, Bushtits and Song and White-crowned Sparrows. In the winter they are joined by Golden-crowned and Fox Sparrows and Ruby-crowned Kinglet. During migration watch for Pacific-slope Flycatcher, Orange-crowned and Wilson's Warblers, and Warbling Vireo.

As the trail reaches its end **Lincoln Park Golf Course** (#7) appears on the right. The open area to the left once had nesting Pygmy Nuthatches and Tree Swallows. Unfortunately, the Park Service cut down the nest trees. From the cliff's edge look east to James D. Phelan Beach, where Long-billed Curlews, Whimbrels, and Marbled Godwits may be among the Willets and Sanderlings on the beach far below.

Before starting up **El Camino Del Mar** (#8), check the first 100 yards of the trail that begins directly across the street and runs along the 18th hole green to Legion of Honor Drive at 43rd Avenue. The pine and cypress trees that line the green may have swallows, nuthatches, Brown Creepers, warblers and possibly Red Crossbills.

There always seems to be bird activity along El Camino Del Mar. Downy Woodpeckers, Olive-sided Flycatchers, Tree Swallows, Pygmy Nuthatches and Dark-eyed Juncos have all nested along the road. In the winter, Yellow-rumped Warblers are abundant, and Townsend's Warblers are fairly common. During migration there may be Nashville, Black-throated Gray and Hermit Warblers. Vagrants like Yellow-throated, Chestnut-sided and Blackpoll Warblers and Northern Parula have been found in the trees along the road. California Quail and Bewick's Wren were once common here. Unfortunately, the large numbers of feral house cats has caused their extirpation in Lincoln Park, as well as throughout most of San Francisco. Walking along El Camino Del Mar it is easy to see why so many ground dwelling birds are in decline.

At the top of the hill above the East Wash, the main road turns in front of the Palace of the Legion of Honor, but you should continue straight along El Camino Del Mar past the dead end sign. The pines that line the street can be quite productive. Red Crossbills have nested here. Warblers in the tops of the trees can be seen more easily by taking the small road to the left where they can be seen at eye level. There are restrooms at the end of this small road.

At the end of El Camino Del Mar a trail leads to the **West Wash** (#4). On a hot day this spot is a must. There is always a trickle of water running through here and the willows can be filled with birds that have come to drink and bathe. During migration this seems to be a favorite stopping place for Pacific-slope Flycatcher, Nashville Warbler, and Lazuli Bunting. Vagrants like Orchard Oriole, Black-throated Green Warbler and Ovenbird have stopped here.

To finish the loop, head straight on to the old El Camino Del Mar road bed. There are usually many common birds along the road until it ends at the parking lot at the east end of El Camino Del Mar. From the northwest corner of the parking lot look for the steps that lead back down to the old trolley car bed. From there retrace your steps to the parking lot at Merrie Way.

A short walk from the Merrie Way parking lot across Point Lobos Avenue to **Sutro Heights Park** (#9) can sometimes be well worth the trip. Once the site of Adolph Sutro's house, the park preserves the look of the original 1880's garden. From the parking lot across from Louie's Restaurant check one of the trails up to the Esplanade. The best birding in the park is along the outside edges of the Esplanade and along Palm Avenue. Although the park does not have the habitat value of the rest of the Lands End, some exciting birds have been found, among them Black-throated Blue and Magnolia Warblers, White-throated and Harris' Sparrows. The eucalyptus snags are favored roosting sites for local Red-tailed and Red-shouldered Hawks. They have also been visited by less common raptors like Broad-winged Hawk, Merlin, and Peregrine Falcon. Hooded Orioles arrive in mid-April and visit the flowering eucalyptus and palms from their neighborhood nest sites. Even on a day with few birds, the breathtaking views from the Esplanade can make birding Sutro Heights Park a pleasure.

It may not always be desirable to do this large loop. By parking at the Legion of Honor smaller loops can be made from the trails that run up and down the washes connecting the upper road and lower trail. From season to season you will find Seal Rocks, Lands End and Lincoln Park ever changing and, for me, ever fascinating.

Directions

From the South Bay, take Interstate 280 north to Skyline Boulevard (Highway 35). Skyline Boulevard becomes the Great Highway near Lake Merced. Follow the Great Highway to the Cliff House. From the north, take Highway 101 through the Presidio to Geary Boulevard and head west. Geary turns into Point Lobos Avenue at about 40th Avenue. Point Lobos Avenue ends in front of the Cliff House; shortly before that is Merrie Way. From the East Bay, take Interstate 80 to Highway 101 towards the Civic Center. This exit ends and becomes Franklin Street. Take Franklin Street to Geary and turn left. Take Geary to Point Lobos Avenue at 40th Avenue and continue to Merrie Way and the Cliff House.

Facilities

There is a Golden Gate National Recreation Area Visitors' Center located on the observation deck at the Cliff House. The Cliff House has a restaurant, snack bar and gift shop. Bathrooms are located next to the snack bar, visitor center, and at the end of the small road next to the Palace Of The Legion Of Honor.

Mary Molteni

Allen's Hummingbird

THE PRESIDIO OF SAN FRANCISCO

❖

Mary Louise Rosegay

Spring ★★★
Summer ★★
Fall ★★★
Winter ★★★

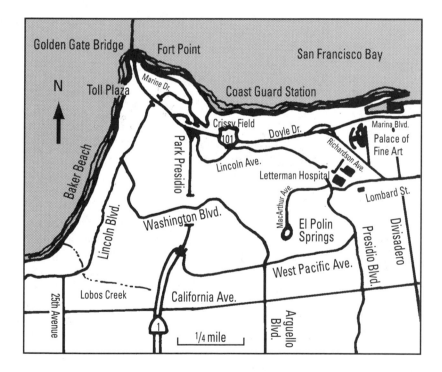

The Presidio of San Francisco is a large park-like area in the northwest corner of the city adjacent to the Golden Gate Bridge. It became a part of the Golden Gate National Recreation Area in 1994. For two centuries it has been a military reservation and, as such, has been inviolate to the spread of urban development. Large tracts were planted with eucalyptus, Monterey cypress, and pine. Other areas, where buildings and homes are clustered, have been planted and landscaped with shrubbery and lawns, all attractive to birds. Like Golden Gate Park, much of the land was originally covered with sand dunes, but there are outcroppings of serpentine with an interesting association of rare plants still growing wild in these places.

Among the special areas for birding in the Presidio, are a small "park within the park" called **El Polin Springs**, off MacArthur Boulevard; **Lobos Creek** at the southwest Lincoln Boulevard Gate, off 25th Avenue; **Baker Beach**, on the shore just west of the Lincoln Boulevard entrance; the San Francisco **Bayshore**, all along the north side of the Presidio; and the wooded hills below Arguello Boulevard.

Like an oasis in the desert, this green community attracts a wide variety of birds. Red-tailed and Red-shouldered Hawks and American Kestrel are known to breed here, and a Peregrine Falcon occasionally flies in for a visit around Baker Beach. Both Great Horned Owl and Western Screech-Owl are residents. Large flocks of California Quail gather to feed through the underbrush and on the wide lawns. These quail are among the very few wild coveys left in the bounds of the city of San Francisco. It is hoped that these precious lands will be protected from the onslaught of feral cats, which have decimated, and even eliminated, most of the quail elsewhere in the city.

In winter, both White-crowned and Golden-crowned Sparrows abound. An occasional White-throated Sparrow has been recorded from these flocks. In spring and early summer the White-crowned Sparrow is one of the most common nesting species, a surprising fact for visiting birders more accustomed to searching out this species in its high mountain breeding habitat.

Other common nesting species are the Mourning Dove, Anna's and Allen's Hummingbirds, Downy Woodpecker, Olive-sided Flycatcher, Scrub Jay, Chestnut-backed Chickadee, Bushtit, Brown Creeper, Pygmy Nuthatch, American Robin, Mockingbird, Hutton's Vireo, Orange-crowned Warbler, California Towhee, Song Sparrow, White-crowned Sparrow, Dark-eyed Junco, Brewer's Blackbird, Purple Finch, House Finch, and Pine Siskin. Wilson's Warblers and Swainson's Thrushes are usually present and probably nest in the area. A pair of Winter Wrens is known to nest in the heavily wooded area below Arguello Boulevard.

One of the rarest species suspected of nesting on or near the Presidio is the Red Crossbill. It has been recorded at all seasons of the year, often with immature individuals in the small flocks. Perhaps the best areas to search for this bird are around the edges of the Presidio golf course and on the slope below the Arguello Boulevard overlook. It has also been seen in the woods between Lincoln Boulevard and Baker Beach on the west side of the Presidio, as well as along Lobos Creek, at the bottom of the Lincoln Boulevard hill.

Since 1966, Hooded Orioles have nested in a small colony near Letterman Hospital, just inside the Lombard Gate. The nests seem to be placed only in the fan-leaf palm here—low-hanging, purse-shaped nests fastened neatly to the underside of the palm leaf and constructed of the fine, tough fibers pulled by the birds from the leaf edges. Originally the nests were found in the palms along Presidio Boulevard at the west end of Lombard Street. More recently, the orioles have moved first to an area by the Lombard Gate, and then westward across the Presidio to Sea Cliff and on toward Lincoln Park, wherever the fan palms are not too closely trimmed. There are usually a number of "dummy" or practice nests in these trees, but quiet, careful watching will reveal the occupied ones. The first birds appear around mid-April, with May perhaps the best month to watch their activities. Northern Mockingbirds also nest in this general area.

Occasional Red-breasted Sapsuckers are found, usually in winter, and Flickers are seen in very large numbers in winter, in meadows such as the one at the ball field beside Lobos Creek. The Hairy Woodpecker is quite rare in this area, but has been suspected of breeding not far from Lobos Creek.

Large flocks of Cedar Waxwings come and go in winter and spring, often feeding in blooming eucalyptus. Both Ruby-crowned Kinglet and Golden-crowned Kinglet, as well as Hermit Thrush, Winter Wren, Townsend's and Yellow-rumped Warblers are not too difficult to see in wooded areas. Even a Hermit Warbler might catch one's eye in winter, or a secretive Varied Thrush.

During spring migration almost anything can happen in such an environment. Western Tanagers can be common, and so can some warblers and vireos. Tennessee Warblers have been seen several times, usually announcing their presence in song, somewhere around El Polin Springs. The Ash-throated Flycatcher, Say's Phoebe, Western Bluebird, Lazuli Bunting and Black-headed Grosbeak, while seldom seen in numbers, can occasionally surprise a birder almost anywhere in the Presidio where there is appropriate cover.

The fall hawk migration can be spectacular over the Presidio. Many of the species recorded from the Point Diablo hawk lookout, at Fort Cronkite, cross over here. Red-tailed, Red-shouldered, and a number of less common buteos are often seen. Among the rarities are Broad-winged Hawks, once thought to be "mistaken calls." Over the last decade or so, they have become more common and over 100 have been counted during the fall migration over the hawk lookout. In good years some numbers of Ferruginous and Rough-legged Hawks may appear. Sharp-shinned and Cooper's Hawks are common and others, such as the Northern Harrier, falcons such as the American Kestrel and the less common Merlin and Peregrine, can be seen over the Presidio. Ospreys are sometimes seen in fairly large numbers and even a Golden Eagle is possible. One of the rarest fall migrants ever recorded on the Presidio was the Clark's Nutcracker. In late October of 1961 a group of at least seven birds appeared and spent some days among the pines on Washington Boulevard where it overlooks the ocean. (Our thanks to Naomi Svenningsen for this interesting record.)

There is much waterfront on the Presidio—from the baylands on the north side around to Fort Point, under the Golden Gate Bridge and thence to the ocean at Baker Beach. Most productive has been the bay side, where cormorants, loons, grebes, Red-breasted Mergansers, Surf Scoters and other ducks may be seen close to shore. Oldsquaw and Harlequin Ducks may appear along the beach just west of the Coast Guard Station along with large numbers of other water birds during the winter herring run. Common Murre, Marbled Murrelet, Parasitic and Pomarine Jaegers, Sooty and Black-vented Shearwaters are more likely to be seen farther out, in the strait beyond the Golden Gate Bridge. Some years have brought tens of thousands of milling Sooty Shearwaters all the way up to the Bridge, feeding for several hours. The time must depend on the tide and the available food, but the season is usually late summer or early fall.

A few lucky birders have seen jaegers pursuing terns along the beach as far into the Bay as the yacht club just east of the Presidio. Forster's Terns are present the year around and Elegant Terns move up from their southern breeding grounds into this area in summer, often in fairly large numbers. Common Terns and Least Terns are sometimes seen in small groups near, or on, the old pier at the Coast Guard Station. Many gull species can be studied to advantage here and on the Crissy Field landing strip nearby. This has proven to be a particularly convenient place to see Thayer's Gull in winter. Others that may gather here in winter are: Western Gull, Glaucous-winged Gull, Herring Gull, California Gull, Ring-billed Gull, Mew Gull, occasionally Bonaparte's Gull, and very rarely, a Glaucous Gull.

Brown Pelicans have become quite common in recent years and large numbers even winter here. When they arrive after breeding in summer, they are accompanied by a retinue of Heermann's Gulls, which find an easy way to feed by following the pelicans as they dive and bring in their catches. White Pelicans may also appear occasionally in small flocks outside the breeding season— always a dramatic sight as they soar by the Golden Gate Bridge and down along the Marina.

Shorebirds, such as Black Turnstone and Sanderling can be common along the shore, especially in stormy weather. Willet, Black-bellied Plover (and even an occasional American Golden-Plover) along with a few others may attract the birder's interest. The Wandering Tattler will sometimes come inside the Bay, but chances are better along the rocks outside the bridge, around Baker Beach and beyond.

Whatever the season, the birder can expect more than the usual city birding while exploring the Presidio. As this book goes to press the details of the future of the Presidio under the National Park Service are still in discussion. But many naturalists are working to reintroduce native plants and to protect the many natural habitats in this most beautiful park. Hopefully, the birds will be protected, and their numbers increase. Over the coming years may it become a peaceful, favorite retreat for us all. Good birding.

Directions

There are several entrances to the Presidio. The main one is the Lombard Gate, off Lombard Street, on the east side of the Presidio. There are regular city buses (Muni) entering and leaving here. Other entrances are off Marina Boulevard and Richardson Avenue. On the south are the Presidio Boulevard and Arguello Boulevard entrances. On the southwest side, the main "back" entrance, off 20th Avenue, is the Lincoln Boulevard entrance. It is a steep climb up the hill to Robbe Avenue and thence to Washington Boulevard. If one continues past Robbe, he will reach the entrance to the Golden Gate Bridge. From here, buses go to and from Marin County. Muni buses also enter the Presidio at Lincoln, near Baker Beach and Lobos Creek.

Fort Point can be reached by a road about one block east of the toll plaza. Paths run from here, eastward, all along the water front. El Polin is a favorite birding area reached from MacArthur Boulevard, off the lower end of Presidio Boulevard.

Directions for reaching the Presidio itself depend on your point of origin, as the entrances are numerous. From the South Bay (San Mateo and Santa Clara counties) take Interstate 280 north. The highway becomes 19th Avenue, passes through Golden Gate Park and continues as Park Presidio. This goes directly to the Golden Gate Bridge toll plaza, where there is a marked right hand turn into the Presidio. Be *very careful* not to miss this turn. If you do, enjoy your drive across the Golden Gate.

To reach the east side of the Presidio, turn off Park Presidio shortly beyond the tunnel and follow Doyle Drive to the Presidio exit. There are two entrances within the block, one directly into the north side, and another, just beyond it, into the main Lombard Gate. Buses come in by the Lombard Gate, and there is a bus stop in front of the Letterman Hospital, one block inside the gate.

From the East Bay, take I-80 across the Bay Bridge, taking the Civic Center-Van Ness Avenue turnoff. Go north on Van Ness to Lombard Street, turn left and follow it to the Presidio Lombard Gate.

From Marin County, take the immediate right-hand exit out of the gate of the Golden Gate Bridge toll plaza. (Be sure to use the right-hand lane to approach the toll booths). This short road leads to Lincoln Boulevard. Near its entrance is a covered **installation map** of the area. Internal maps are available at the Army Museum near the intersection of Lincoln and Funston. New ones will, no doubt, be distributed as the Golden Gate National Recreation Area takes over the Presidio.

Facilities

There are restrooms at the Army Museum, and in the buildings housing the PX and Commissary, not far from the Bayshore. There is at present, a cafeteria, just behind the Post Office in the center of the Presidio, and a small grocery not far inside the entrance from Doyle Drive. Gas stations are plentiful in the Marina and in the Richmond district, at the south end of the Presidio.

Mary Molteni

American Robin (fledgling)

LAKE MERCED

❖

Dan Murphy

Spring ★★★★
Summer ★★
Fall ★★★★ (Best)
Winter ★★★★

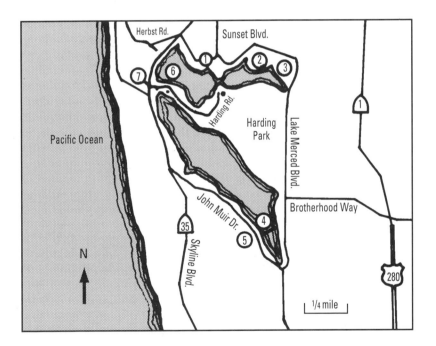

Lake Merced is probably San Francisco's single most productive birding area. Its variety of habitats and its proximity to the ocean provide an ever-varying avian population. Located in the southwest corner of the city, it attracts large numbers of residents and migrants between September and May. Summer birding tends to be limited as to species, but these include summering Clark's Grebes and Bank Swallows from the nearby colony at Fort Funston.

Terryl Graves

Western Grebe

North Lake

The area around **Sunset Circle** (#1), a large parking lot at the southern end of Sunset Boulevard, provides excellent birding opportunities. From the circle check the eucalyptus trees to the west for spring and Fall migrants. Breeding species for this area include Red-shouldered Hawk, American Kestrel, Allen's and Anna's Hummingbirds, Downy Woodpecker, Black Phoebe, Tree Swallow, Bushtit, Orange-crowned and Wilson's Warblers, White-crowned and Song Sparrows, and House and Purple Finches. Migrants and winter residents are likely to include Cedar Waxwings, Ruby-crowned Kinglets, Townsend's and Yellow-rumped Warblers and, more rarely, Merlins, Summer Tanagers, Northern Orioles and other rarities. April brings in an occasional Rufous Hummingbird. The several trails leading to a small fishing beach pass through habitat favored by these and many other species.

Be sure to check the willows around the edge of the field above the beach for warblers and flycatchers. Tropical Kingbirds have wintered here and Western Kingbirds may be seen during spring migration. Check the lake for Western and Clark's Grebes, Double-crested Cormorants and other assorted waterfowl and gulls. At the paved path continue to the right and down the hill to where a bridge connects this area to Harding Golf Course. Check the willows and marsh as you walk out to this site. This is an excellent vantage point from which to view the marsh. Watch the shoreline for Green Herons, Black-crowned Night-Herons, Soras, Virginia Rails, Marsh Wrens, Common Yellowthroats and Song Sparrows. This can be a particularly charming area at dawn and dusk when ducks fly over and rails call from the reeds.

Return to the parking lot and walk east along the bike path, continue beyond the cove to a **large flat field** (#2), then turn right along the dirt path. Check the weeds for House Finches and White-crowned and Golden-crowned Sparrows. The coastal scrub in this area has provided winter habitat for Blue-gray Gnatcatchers and Palm Warblers. Various warblers, Ruby-crowned Kinglets and occasionally a Bewick's Wren can be found in or near the cypress grove on the right. Just beyond the grove scan the shore line below for grebes, ducks, waders and gulls. A Black Phoebe can usually be seen in this area. Continue along the path occasionally checking the shoreline until you reach the eucalyptus grove. The grove holds birds similar to those in the grove near Sunset Circle. Just beyond the grove check the eastern end of the lake. Ruddy Ducks and Pied-billed Grebes usually predominate, but watch for Northern Shovelers, Cinnamon Teal, Greater Scaup and Canvasbacks during winter and spring. Great Egrets, Great Blue Herons and Black-crowned Night-Herons can often be seen in the marshes in this area.

Continue on to the paved path and follow it eastward beyond the large willow grove to a road which is usually blocked by a large log. Take the **obstructed road** (#3) down into the cypresses and check the grove for Pygmy Nuthatches, Brown Creepers, Chestnut-backed Chickadees and warblers. Look in the tangled vegetation on the edge of this area for Bewick's Wrens, Lincoln's Sparrows (winter), Purple Finches and a variety of other birds, particularly during migration. Continue east along the road by the willow grove to the end. Black Phoebe, Pacific-slope Flycatcher, Orange-crowned and Wilson's Warblers, and Purple Finch can often be found here during breeding season and migration. Winter may bring a glimpse of a Hermit Thrush, a Varied Thrush or a Fox Sparrow. From here return to the circle.

South Lake

From the circle drive right (west) on Lake Merced Boulevard for about 2 miles, all the way around the southern end of the lake and then north along the west side of the lake to the parking area by the **concrete bridge** (#4). When water levels are normal water will pass under the bridge, but drought and tapping of the aquifer have dropped the lake's level so low it seems unlikely the lake will return to historic levels for some time.

The area near the concrete bridge provides habitat for as many as 300 Brown-headed Cowbirds from September through March. Brewer's and Red-winged Blackbirds are common too. Tricolored Blackbirds have been found here and there are even a few records of Yellow-headed Blackbirds. White-crowned Sparrows and House Finches are resident and are joined by Golden-crowned Sparrows by October. In the small lake to the south watch for Mew and Ring-billed Gulls as well as all the other common gulls of our area. Ducks should include Mallards, Green-winged Teal, Ring-neckeds, Ruddies and a few others. The marshes here are home to Marsh Wrens, Common Yellowthroats, and Song Sparrows. Swamp (rare in winter), Lincoln's (regular in winter) and Savannah Sparrows can often be found in the marshes around the edge of this impoundment. Watch for hummingbirds in the willows. If you walk to the south end of the lake note the Red-winged Blackbird colony in the willow grove. They displaced Marsh Wrens in this area and are the only breeding colony on the lake. If water conditions permit, you may see Common Snipe along the marsh's edge and Killdeer on the beaches and open mudflats. Fall can produce exciting shorebirds if the water level is low enough to expose unvegetated lake bottom. Western and Least Sandpipers have been joined by Semipalmated and Pectoral Sandpipers in recent years. A Curlew Sandpiper made a fall appearance and a Solitary Sandpiper was a spring visitor. Shorebirds generally do not winter here. North of the bridge watch for all local waterfowl species including sea ducks and loons after storms and during migration. The marshes on both sides of the bridge host Great Blue Heron, Great and Snowy Egrets, and Black-crowned Night-Herons. Green Herons court over the lake in spring and nest in willow groves. American Bittern, once fairly common, may return if the lake's water level is ever stabilized and marshes are permitted to mature.

The open water in the lake to the north of the bridge can produce interesting birds all year. Look in the cover along the lake's edge for grebes and ducks. The open water is good for Clark's, Western, Horned, Eared and Pied-billed Grebes. It is also a place to check for loons, sea ducks, mergansers and vagrant terns and gulls, particularly after storms and during migration. Just to the north of the bridge on both the east and west shores are fishing piers which should be checked for rails and other marsh birds. The concrete bridge is an especially good place to watch swallows. From February through September, Tree, Violet-green, Cliff, Barn, Rough-winged and Bank Swallows feed over the lake and marshes in this area. All nest locally, with the Cliff Swallows nesting on the bridge itself. Spring and fall should give a glimpse of an Osprey or two among the gulls and other raptors which soar overhead.

❖ **Tip** *Two small marshes west of the bridge area are great places to practice swallow identification. A half hour there can make you an expert on differentiating between Rough-winged, Bank and immature Tree Swallows.*

Just across John Muir Drive and a bit west of the concrete bridge A you'll find a **poorly birded vagrant trap** (#5). Walk north along the concrete drainage ditch to check the oaks, willows, cypress, pines and especially the flowering eucalyptus. A flock of migrant insectivores can usually be found here. Listen for the calling Pygmy Nuthatches and warblers which will mark the feeding flock. It can be expected to include a dozen or so species and sometimes it includes vagrants such as Canada Warblers, Northern Parulas, Blackpoll Warblers, American Redstarts and Summer Tanagers. This area is well isolated and infrequently birded, so its real value as a vagrant trap is not yet fully appreciated.

The Boathouse

Drive north on John Muir Drive to its intersection with Skyline and continue north around the lake to the entrance road marked Lake Merced, **Harding Park** (#6). Park near the boathouse. Restrooms, a bar and a restaurant are located in the building. If you wish to fish or bird from a boat, rentals are available here as well.

The shoreline is frequented by the previously mentioned herons and egrets. The piers usually host a large flock of Western Gulls. Double-crested Cormorants roost in the trees and fish the lake, much to the consternation of fishermen. The wires in this area are used by all of our swallow species for resting, particularly during migration. Bank Swallows can usually be found here between April and July. From the south-facing piers walk west along the shoreline. Check the marsh by the children's fishing pier for nesting Marsh Wrens, Common Yellowthroats and Song Sparrows. They are often joined in fall and winter by Fox, Lincoln's and Swamp Sparrows. Continue to the end of the path where it ends at the fenced **pump station** (#7). Downy Woodpeckers, Black Phoebes, Chestnut-backed Chickadees and Common Bushtits nest near here. The eucalyptus grove is deteriorating, but it remains a valuable resource for wintering birds and a potential vagrant trap. Here you can see an exotic habitat, composed of eucalyptus, *Albizzia* and other weedy species which attract vagrants in migration and hold them through the winter. This habitat mix occurs elsewhere around the northern and western shores of the lake and should be checked for vagrants too. Species seen in these areas not only include the expected wintering Orange-crowned, Yellow and Townsend's Warblers, but Tennessee and Black-and-White Warblers, Northern Waterthrushes, Northern Parulas, Western Tanagers, Summer Tanagers and Northern Orioles. These areas also provide breeding habitat for Yellow and Wilson's Warbler and an occasional Northern Oriole.

The beach and open waters of the North Lake should be checked for shorebirds, ducks and gulls. Heermann's, Thayer's, Mew, Glaucous-winged, Herring, California, Western and Bonaparte's Gulls all occur on the lake at one time or another during the year. Five species of grebes winter in this area, while spring and fall will provide the opportunity to see migrating Red-necked and Red Phalaropes.

The trees at the edge of the golf course provide breeding habitat for Downy Woodpeckers, Tree Swallows, Common Ravens, Pygmy Nuthatches, Brown Creepers, American Robins, Brewer's Blackbirds, and House Finches. It is best not to attempt to bird Harding Golf Course, which is usually crowded and golfers are under pressure to keep moving and unlikely to look charitably on intruding birders. The road continues to the club house where there is another restaurant and bar. The newly-constructed Harding Park Pedestrian Bridge connects the golf course area to the Sunset Circle.

Hiking

For those not interested in driving there are several alternatives. The 4.6 Mile walk around the lake can be broken up by birding at the spots described above. The mile or so along the east side of Harding Park is the only long stretch devoid of bird life. The half mile walk around the southern end of the lake from the concrete bridge to the south end of the lake and back around the other side can easily produce a list of 25 or more species almost any time of the year. The footbridge connecting the Sunset Circle with Harding Park enables walkers to follow roads and bike paths around the north and western parts of the North Lake. This 2 mile walk can provide a list of 30 or more species almost any time of the year.

Directions

Located in San Francisco, Lake Merced is at the south end of Sunset Blvd. and the west end of Brotherhood Way. From the south bayshore and central areas of the peninsula, take Interstate 280 north to Highway One (stay in the three left lanes of 280) and continue about a mile north. Exit at Brotherhood Way westbound. Follow Brotherhood Way about 1 mile west to Lake Merced. From the south coast follow Skyline Boulevard (Hwy. 35) north past the Westlake exits into San Francisco and to the west side of Lake Merced. From the north take Highway One south through Golden Gate Park, turn right onto Lincoln Way (the street bordering the park on the south), drive west to Sunset Blvd. (between 36th & 37th Avenues.), then left onto Sunset for about 2.5 miles to the lake. From downtown or the East Bay take the freeway, Hwy. 101, south to Hwy. 280. Go south on 280 to the Alemeny Exit and get in the right lane for a turn onto Alemeny (the first major intersection). Go west past the stop light to Brotherhood Way and follow it just over a mile west to the lake.

FORT FUNSTON

❖

Dan Murphy

Spring ★★★
Summer ★★
Fall ★★★
Winter ★★

San Francisco's Fort Funston is located at the southwest corner of the city. This area of coastal bluffs and rolling dunes provides a contiguous open space between the ocean and Lake Merced. Its vegetation incorporates groves of eucalyptus and cypress trees. *Albizzia, Myoporum,* German Ivy, and a number of other invasive weedy intruders along with a rich blend of California native plants comprise the understory. To the birder it offers two exciting and distinct opportunities. The upland dunes and islands of trees come alive during the fall and spring. The ocean and the southern sections of beach can be incredibly rich at any time of year. North along Ocean Beach birding is less productive, but it can be interesting from time to time.

The Uplands

August through October is probably the preferred time to visit Fort Funston's upland dunes. Access is best from southbound Skyline Boulevard (Hwy. 35). From San Francisco drive south on Skyline past Lake Merced. Up the hill to the right turn into Fort Funston. From the south drive north into San Francisco on Skyline to the stop light at the bottom of the hill (John Muir Drive), make a U-turn, then return to the top of the hill and turn right on to the access road. Turn right at the intersection and continue to the far end of the parking lot.

Except under the most adverse weather conditions you will find yourself sharing the parking lot with hang-glider enthusiasts. The bluffs over the ocean here are the most favored spot in Northern California for this sport. A hang glider viewing platform has been constructed southwest of the parking lot and provides an excellent view of the ocean below. From here check the ocean for flocks of feeding birds which may include Brown Pelicans, Brandt's Cormorants, Western and Heermann's Gulls as well as Forster's, Elegant and Caspian Terns. There is always the chance of a Pomarine or Parasitic Jaeger, particularly during late summer and fall. Although few birds stop in the shrubs near the overlook, this scrub growth has attracted vagrants, notably a Sedge Wren and a Blackburnian Warbler. Killdeer, blackbirds and American Pipits can be found along any of the trails at Fort Funston.

The Sunset Trail, beginning at the northwest corner of the parking lot, leads to the best birding areas. From the parking lot follow the trail north to its fork, then right around the east side of Battery Davis.

At **Battery Davis** check the trees for warblers. Eastern species, including Blackpoll, Chestnut-sided, and Tennessee Warblers and American Redstarts, and the more common Orange-crowned, Yellow, Black-throated Gray, Nashville, Wilson's, Townsend's', and Yellow-rumped warblers can be found in fall and, to a lesser degree, in spring. Warbling, Hutton's and Solitary Vireos are also expected at one time or another during migration. Mourning Doves, Tree Swallows and Chestnut-backed Chickadees nest here.

From the middle entrance to Battery Davis go down the hill to the right. keep an eye on the cypress groves and the *Albizzia* (the large fern-leafed shrubs) for flycatchers, warblers and sparrows. The grove at the fork, appropriately known as **The Y Grove**, should be birded carefully. Allen's Hummingbirds, Bewick's Wrens, Brown Creepers and White-crowned Sparrows nest near here. Fall insectivore flocks can be expected to include the same species mentioned in connection with Battery Davis. The coffeeberry shrubs on the hillside behind the north part of this grove provide berries for migrating Western Tanagers and White-crowned Sparrows during September. After checking this area carefully walk south (to the right) on the path as it descends past this grove and on to the next one. Check the shrubs between the cypress covered bunker and the eucalyptus grove farthest south. A large insectivore flock here was once found to include a Prairie Warbler. Though highly variable as a birding site, this may prove to be an area significant to migrants and the vagrants which accompany them. After checking this area return to the Y Grove and make your way to the right over the dunes to the cypress and eucalyptus grove which parallels Skyline Boulevard

Skyline Grove is perhaps the richest migrant trap at Fort Funston. This grove offers the greatest diversity in terms of vegetation and thus in terms of birds. It can be accessed by crossing the dunes on any of a number of informal trails or bridle paths. The best areas are openings where light penetrates the grove and ecotones (areas where two major vegetation types blend together).

Watch for all our common migrants and vagrants. Eastern Kingbird, Red-eyed Vireo, Black-throated Blue Warbler, Black-throated Green Warbler, and Clay-colored Sparrow are only a few of the vagrants which have been recorded here. Allen's Hummingbird, Downy Woodpecker, Tree Swallow, Bewick's Wren, Pygmy Nuthatch, Brown Creeper, Common Raven and White-crowned Sparrow nest in the grove. As you return to the parking lot keep an eye on the adjacent dunes for feeding flocks, any of which may include interesting birds from time to time.

To the south of the parking lot are some rather attractive areas which are not generally birded. The abandoned golf course just south of Fort Funston remains the private property of the Olympic Club. A number of so far unfulfilled plans call for it to be turned over to the National Park Service in exchange for land owned by the city of San Francisco. So far, this three-way transaction remains hostage to budgets and bureaucracy. If this land ever is opened to the public it will offer some very interesting birding opportunities. Other groves of trees south of the parking lot also provide opportunities to see vagrants.

The Beach

The beach is most easily reached from the Great Highway just south of Sloat Boulevard. Use the southernmost parking lot, about a tenth of a mile south of the Sloat Boulevard. Access can also be made from the upland dunes by a trail through the gully just north of Battery Davis or by walking to the north end of the paved Sunset Trail and then following the dunes to the north end of the sand bluffs.

The primary attraction at Fort Funston's beach is the **Bank Swallow colony.** Located in the sand bluffs just south of the parking lot, this colony of more than one hundred burrows is active from April through July. This is the northern-most major Bank Swallow colony on the California coast. The birds feed over nearby Lake Merced and illustrate the ecological link between the adjoining areas.

The beach itself is a major resting area for migrating shorebirds in spring and fall. It is an excellent spot to see alternate (breeding) plumage Black-bellied Plover, Marbled Godwit, Willet, Sanderling, and other spring migrants. The offshore waters are quite interesting as well. From the parking lot, the beach or any of the bluffs look for all three loons, Western and Clark's Grebes, our three cormorants, Brown Pelicans, the three scoters including the locally rare Black, and all local gulls and terns. Mixed flocks of frenzied seabirds follow striped bass runs into the surf. The bass hit bait fish from below and the birds take them from above. The feeding flock may include all the previously mentioned species plus Sooty Shearwaters, Pomarine Jaegers and Parasitic Jaegers. The best time to witness feeding frenzies is on incoming summer tides within about 2 hours of high tide. Millions of Sooty Shearwaters patrol the coast between June and September and their feeding frenzies can be awesome. A telescope is usually needed to distinguish other shearwaters from the masses of Sooties but on occasion they will be close enough to distinguish them with the naked eye.

Summer can be a pretty good time at **Ocean Beach** north of Fort Funston. A walk along the beach for a couple of miles can produce some interesting sightings both in the surf and resting on the dunes. Heermann's and Western Gulls are most common. Be sure to check all the flocks since some of them will be composed of Caspian, Elegant and Forster's Terns. Common and Arctic Terns show up in small numbers late in the season. Shorebirds form huge resting flocks on the beach. They can often be seen near the new section of seawall north of Taraval Street. The walking path which follows The Great Highway is a better observation point than the beach itself, particularly at the seawall. If you use the path be sure to watch for Killdeer, American Kestrels and Western Meadowlarks.

Winter birding is a bit slower along the beach. A Thayer's Gull can often be found among the small resting flocks of gulls between Fort Funston and the end of the beach about three miles to the north. Snowy Plovers occur at two locations along the beach. Look for a small flock about a block or two north of Sloat Boulevard. A second small flock can generally be found between Noriega and Irving Streets. This area is accessible from the Lower Great Highway at Judah Street. Look for the Snowy Plovers in the upland dunes among wind-blown litter. They are seldom found on the wave washed areas that Sanderlings favor.

BIRDING SMALL PARKS AND OTHER POINTS OF INTEREST IN SAN FRANCISCO

❖

Dan Murphy

San Francisco offers many fine birding sites besides it's large parks. Virtually any park with a wooded edge can be expected to yield birds at one time of the year or another. Here are a few neighborhood sites. In addition to these you can bird parks such as Buena Vista, Mt. Davidson, Golden Gate Heights, Walton Square, Twin Peaks and Sutro Heights; or other spots—Pier 98, the Embarcadero, the Russian Hill Steps, Fort Mason, the unused reservoir across the street from City College of San Francisco and the grounds of the Laguna Honda Home.

The Zoo located in the southwest corner of the City on Sloat Boulevard, has some potential as a birding site. Officially known as the San Francisco Zoological Gardens, it is most productive on weekdays and in the early morning. Don't even think about it on pleasant weekend days or on the first Wednesday of the month (free day) when large crowds are attracted. Just walking the paths, particularly by the many paddocks, will provide a rich variety of birds at almost any season. Most breeding species found in the city's parks can be found here as well. Winter provides an opportunity to pick up a vagrant or two. A spot which is particularly interesting is the untended area to the east of the Grizzly Bear enclosure. A Black-and-white Warbler and an Ovenbird have been found here, and there are usually a few more common, but interesting, birds in this unique little spot. The ponds which are home to a number of exotic species are often used by wintering ducks, gulls and other water birds. Waders—including Cattle Egrets—often invade the zoo's water habitats. The blackbird flocks should be checked for Tricolored and Yellow-headed Blackbirds.

The Sigmund Stern Grove And Pine Lake Park are located at 19th Avenue and Sloat Boulevard and continue west to about 34th Avenue. A parking lot at the end of Vale Avenue (off Sloat Boulevard) is the best place to park. Winter and spring are the preferred times to bird these parks. The steep terrain of the canyon walls and the tall eucalyptus trees which dominate the areas make birding in the wooded sections very difficult. Winter birds can usually be found feeding on the ground, in lower branches of blooming eucalyptus trees or feeding on fruiting shrubs. Breeding birds are much harder to find since many inhabit the forest canopy which is often not visible from the ground.

From the parking lot at the foot of Vale walk west through the meadow. The shrubs on the left (south) edge of the meadow are good for all local sparrows and usually a wintering White-throated Sparrow can be found there. The eucalyptus to the right bloom in winter and are an excellent winter habitat for insectivores which have included a Dusky-capped Flycatcher, a Summer Tanager and large numbers of warblers. Red-tailed Hawks usually winter here and Red-shouldered Hawks and Great Horned Owls are permanent residents. Flickers and robins are sometimes numerous on the meadow. At the west end of the meadow a walk around the pond may yield a duck or two. (Be sure to watch for insectivores in the willows around the lake.) Stop at any blooming eucalyptus and expect just about anything. The grasses at the lake's edge can be a good spot for sparrows including Lincoln's (winter).

East of the parking lot it is necessary to bird most of the area by ear. You can find Winter Wrens along the south side of the road in the dense underbrush and warblers near the edges of the meadows in small feeding flocks. One spot which frequently seems to have an interesting bird population is the roadway at the base of the hill beyond the outdoor stage. The eucalyptus blooms here during the early winter and a number of fruiting shrubs add to its attraction. A path through the redwood grove leads to a meadow which should be checked. From there go back to the building (The Tracadero House). Bird the hill behind this for a nice variety of wintering birds. Take any of the various trails back to the parking lot.

Glen Park is located at O'Shaughnessy Boulevard and Elk Street. This little canyon combines a eucalyptus stand and a riparian woodland at the canyon bottom. A trail follows both sides of the creek and offers interesting spring and winter birding. Watch for Red-tailed Hawks, Downy Woodpeckers, Tree Swallows, Pygmy Nuthatches, Brown Creepers, Warbling Vireos, Orange-crowned Warblers, Wilson's Warblers, Song Sparrows, White-crowned Sparrows and Lesser Goldfinches, all of which breed there. Western Tanagers, Black-headed Grosbeaks and Lazuli Buntings are recorded in most years. Other migrants, and even a few vagrants like Black-and-white Warbler and American Redstart have been observed. If this park were birded more frequently it is likely it would produce some very interesting birds.

McLaren Park is a little-birded area that can provide some interesting birds. This is one of the parks which is best not birded alone. Try the riparian area and the ponds off Shelly Boulevard for the widest variety of birds. It is one of the surest places in the city to find Western Meadowlark, Lesser Goldfinch and American Goldfinch. Expect most of the same species as elsewhere in the city. The wooded areas near the open grasslands make this a pretty good park for raptors, particularly in winter. Loggerhead Shrikes were once a sure thing here but they have disappeared from the open areas of this park as well as from other

Dan Keller

American Kestral

parks in the city. Redwood groves should be checked for wintering Hermit and Varied Thrushes. Eucalyptus groves often have winter blooming trees and can be expected to provide habitat for a wide variety of insectivores.

Aquatic Park, located at the foot of Van Ness Avenue, provides a window on the Bay. It is best birded by first checking the little park at the end of Van Ness. Check for many of our woodland species. Hummingbirds are usually around. Parrots—escaped cage birds and their offspring—can often be found in the trees above this area. Check the tall buildings in the neighborhood for a perching Merlin or Peregrine Falcon. The trees by the fast food stand provide day roosting cites for Black-crowned Night-Herons. When that area has been checked walk the length of the fishing pier. Look for gulls and terns, particularly Bonaparte's Gull and Forster's and Caspian Terns. Brandt's and Double-crested

Cormorants are most common, but Pelagic Cormorant can usually be seen flying over the bay or sitting on a nearby pier. Loons, Western and Clark's Grebes, Brown Pelicans, White-winged and Surf Scoters and quite a few other species can be seen from here as well.

Candlestick State Park is located at the southeastern corner of the city and is accessible from Highway 101. Be sure not to waste your time trying to bird this area if there is a baseball or football game at 3COM Park (the stadium). Special events scheduled for the off season are a problem too. This area is best not birded alone.

At low tide between September and April it is possible to see most of our local shorebirds on the mudflats along the entrance road and in the protected cove north of Candlestick Point. The open water is usually good for diving ducks including scaups, scoters, Common Goldeneyes, Buffleheads and Red-breasted Mergansers. Watch for Western, Clark's, Horned and Eared Grebes, all of our loons and all our cormorants. There is also an effort to establish a population of Burrowing Owl here.

Birding at the stadium is pretty slow, but a list of half a dozen or so is likely. White-throated Swifts appear from April through July. A Red-tailed Hawk usually soars over the park at least once during a day game. During migration expect an Osprey to check out the game and look for a Barn Owl passing by during a night game.

Sunset Reservoir is bounded by Quintera on the north, Ortega on the south, 24th Avenue on the east and 28th Avenue on the west. This is a prime winter gull watching spot. The reservoir is covered with a blacktop roof and birds roost on it in large flocks. It should be birded with a scope from 24th Avenue and Quintera or down either street for about a block. During winter expect to see hundreds of Killdeer and Black-bellied Plovers. There is usually a large flock of Mew, California, Ring-billed, Glaucous-winged, Western, Herring and Thayer's gulls. Even though the flock most frequently numbers a few hundred, it sometimes grows to over a thousand. During a December herring run on San Francisco Bay, as many as 96 Thayer's Gulls have been counted resting on this reservoir. Of interest may be the fact this is the only site in San Francisco at which a Snowy Owl has ever been recorded. Other black top reservoirs around the city can be expected to yield similar species.

SAN BRUNO MOUNTAIN

❖

John "Mac" McCormick

Spring ★★★
Summer ★
Fall ★★★★
Winter ★★

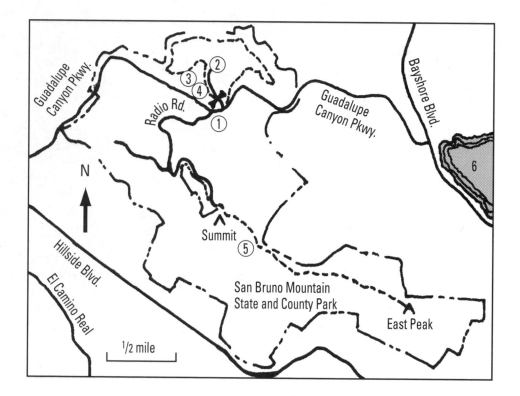

In the fall many birders spend considerable time and expense in frantic trips to such well known vagrant traps as Point Reyes. However, with a much smaller investment of time and money, they can spend a rewarding day of vagrant-hunting practically in their own back yard. In fact, this nearby birding spot can be enjoyed any time of the year.

San Bruno Mountain is located at the border of San Mateo and San Francisco counties, but lies entirely in San Mateo County. It extends approximately two thirds of the way across the peninsula in a southeast to northwest direction. The mountain is actually two parallel ridges, a main ridge with a summit of 1314 feet and a lower ridge known as Guadalupe Hills just to the north. At the southeast extent of the mountain the ridge plunges into San Francisco Bay at Sierra Point. To the northwest, the ridge ends in the urban sprawl of Daly City.

The ridges are crossed by innumerable hiking trails and contain many micro-habitats so that an entire book could be devoted to this one mountain. I have selected two walks that offer the best birding with the hope that you will take the time to explore other areas on this fascinating urban mountain.

The **Saddle Walk** is best if you only have a morning to spend. The saddle area between the ridges was established as a state and county park in 1985. There is a fee ($3.00 at the time we went to press), but only on weekends, and the park has the best birding habitat on the mountain. The area was once a dairy farm and many cypress and eucalyptus were planted as windbreaks. Today, these mature trees provide excellent habitat for resident and migrating birds. A bog and nearby intermittent stream and their accompanying willows provides habitat diversity. Unlike other areas on the mountain this walk is level and is ideal for birders of all ages and physical condition.

Leave the **parking area** (#1) and take the service road north toward the **Edward Bacciocco, Jr. Day Camp** (#2). During the spring, this road provides great birding. Look in the brambles, cypress and eucalyptus that border this route for nesting Northern Orioles, Winter Wrens, Purple Finches, Wrentits, Song Sparrows, Pine Siskins, several warbler species, Olive-sided Flycatchers, an amazing number of Allen's Hummingbirds and other local breeding birds. Spring migrants in this stretch have included Western Tanagers, Black-headed Grosbeaks, Ash-throated Flycatchers, Varied Thrushes, and Warbling Vireos. Even a small flock of Lawrence's Goldfinches, which normally shun the coast for the dryer inland areas, and a high-altitude loving Hammond's Flycatcher have been spotted along the road. In the fall you can expect anything along this road, including some very edible blackberries; a true birding bonus. At the Day Camp turn-around, check the willows and blackberries on both sides of the road. Spring birds here have included Lazuli Buntings, Lark Sparrows, Willow Flycatchers, and ten species of warblers, including a Northern Parula. Occasional flocks of Red Crossbills have been observed in the nearby cypress.

In the Fall, this area has produced a White-throated Sparrow, a Yellow-breasted Chat, and a Rose-breasted Grosbeak. If you follow the trail past the turnaround, you enter into a flat grassland and shrub area dominated by gorse. California Quail, California Towhees, White-crowned Sparrows and Song Sparrows nest here. Northern Mockingbirds forage over the grasslands and a Grasshopper Sparrow was seen in the gorse in 1991. In the boggy areas you can hear the Common Yellowthroat defending its territory. In wet years, a small pond has been a nesting site for a pair of Mallards and a winter home for a pair of Common Snipe. Occasionally glance upward and you may be rewarded with a view of one of the many raptors that sail over this area. Northern Harriers, White-tailed Kites, Red-shouldered Hawks, Merlins, Osprey as well as a resident pair of Red-tailed Hawks have frequented the area.

From here backtrack to the parking lot and take the **Old Guadalupe Trail** (#3). This road splits what is called the Fog Forest, a very damp area that is home to many Winter Wrens. In May and June you are serenaded by the ethereal song of Swainson's Thrush as well as those of many nesting warblers. Look for the nesting Red-tailed Hawks high in the cypresses. A wintering American Redstart was found feeding among the Leather Ferns growing on the cypress trunks here on a Christmas Count. Another American Redstart was discovered further along the trail one spring.

Continue along the trail past the connecting Bog Trail until you reach the stretch of the trail bordered by acacia shrubs. Take some time here, especially in the spring. One late April morning, a single 20 foot acacia shrub produced 7 species of warblers at one time (including a Hermit, Black-throated Gray and Yellow Warblers). In the same area a spring Gray Flycatcher proved to be only the third county record for this bird. It is an excellent habitat for Empidonax flycatchers in general. Search the adjacent eucalyptus grove in the spring for Western Tanagers and Ash-throated Flycatchers. Many migrants and resident birds take advantage of the abundant insect life found on the acacia.

Follow the Old Guadalupe Trail through a large grove of eucalyptus (noted for Great Horned Owls and wintering Cedar Waxwings) or backtrack to the **Bog Trail** (#4). The Bog Trail loops around a small creek with a quarter mile stand of willows. It is a perfect way to end the hike. In the spring, nesting Orange-crowned and Wilson's Warblers abound here, and migrant MacGillivray's Warblers may be seen. Once again, the singing of the Swainson's Thrush fills the air as does the song of the nesting Purple Finch. You can expect to find all the spring and summer resident riparian birds of the Bay Area in these willows with an occasional surprise, like the summer record of the especially rare Hooded Warbler. Since then I can not walk past these willows in the spring and fall without the great anticipation of finding a particularly intriguing rare species.

As you return to the parking lot in the spring, you should be able to hear singing Common Yellowthroats below you in the bog, and in the fall, Lincoln's Sparrows are found in the baccharis. If you are very lucky, you may spy a secretive Green-tailed Towhee scurrying through the brush. There are only two records of this high desert bird from San Mateo County, both on San Bruno Mountain. One of those sightings was made here near the parking area.

Walking the **Main Ridge** (#5) is truly an exhilarating experience. After you enter the park, turn left, drive under the parkway and continue to a parking area at the summit of the main ridge. From this vantage point the entire San Francisco Bay Area is at your feet and the view is spectacular. From the parking area, take the trail east. This runs along the entire length of the ridge until its end above the community of Brisbane. Birds along this walk are typical of the coastal scrub; Rufous-sided Towhees, Bewick's Wrens, California Towhees, Song Sparrows and Scrub Jays with resident raptors such as Red-tailed Hawks and American Kestrels above and Hermit Thrushes and Fox Sparrows in the winter. But during the fall and spring migrations be ready for quite a variety of unusual species. Observations during the spring have produced as many as thirty-three Ospreys, a rare Northern Goshawk, numerous Sharp-shinned and Cooper's Hawks, a Prairie Falcon and even a very unusual adult Bald Eagle. A pair of Northern Harriers have nested on the north slope just below the buildings at the extreme northwest end of the ridge. The fall raptor migration doesn't produce the numbers typical of Point Diablo and Hill 129 in the Marin Headlands, but a morning spent watching raptors from the ridge will provide both the expected migrants and a few surprises, like a Broad-winged Hawk, a dark phase Ferruginous Hawk, Merlins or Golden Eagles all of which have been observed in previous years. Keep your eyes and ears open for migrating passerine species, especially in the fall. Several species of swifts have been seen and heard, as well as unusual coastal migrants like Evening Grosbeaks and Purple Martins. A migrant White-faced Ibis was once seen circling the summit several times before heading south. The easternmost half of the ridge is open grassland habitat with wintering flocks of Horned Larks—otherwise rare in San Mateo County—and Western Meadowlarks with an occasional White-tailed Kite hovering overhead. A particular surprise was a winter record Sage Thrasher observed on the ridge trail above Brisbane. The gullies on the southeast slope have harbored Rock Wrens and the canyons sloping to the northeast have had wintering Blue-gray Gnatcatchers. The two prominent canyons just west of Brisbane are Buckeye and Owl Canyons and are noted for a remnant coast live oak woodland, including live oak, California Bay, Holly Cherry, and California Buckeye. Unless you have a high tolerance for Poison Oak and an excellent cardiovascular system these canyons are best explored by approaching cross country from Brisbane rather than dropping down from the ridge trail. The two canyons are not heavily birded, but should be!

At this point, (unless you have left a second car parked along Old Bayshore or you are particularly adventuresome) you must retrace your steps back to the summit parking lot.

A word of caution is necessary for the Ridge Trail. Mornings can be deceptively warm, but a strong and cool afternoon breeze can make the return trip a bit uncomfortable. Take a jacket.

If the winter weather turns particularly windy and cold on the mountain, you can retreat eastward to the **Brisbane Lagoon** (#6), which is usually sheltered, and enjoy a morning watching shorebirds. Good numbers of Semipalmated Plovers, Western and Least Sandpipers, Dowitchers, Willets, Egrets and even a Whimbrel or two feed on the mudflats at low tide. There are plenty of bay ducks to be observed and very rarely, a Tundra Swan or visiting Peregrine Falcon has added to the mix. A late fall Mountain Bluebird visited the area for a day, its brilliant splash of blue brightening the drab pre-winter colors. Burrowing Owls have been seen in the adjacent grasslands, but recent grading in the area has displaced them. For you masochists, there are plenty of gulls to sort through, many of them obviously hybrids.

Botany

One would be remiss in not mentioning the spectacular wildflower display San Bruno Mountain puts on in the spring. From late February to well into May the mountain is a botanist's delight. Some of the plants are endemic to San Bruno Mountain and others are rare or endangered everywhere else in the Bay Area. The open areas are a riot of color. In addition to the flowers, you may get fleeting glimpses of the Mission Blue and the San Bruno Elfin, two of the four endangered butterflies you might encounter on your walk. Both depend on the endemic flora of San Bruno Mountain for their survival. In the spring, it is wise to bring your camera as well as your binoculars.

Directions

There are two access routes to the park: east and west.

Eastern Access If you're traveling from the south on Highway 101 take the Brisbane turnoff and travel north on Old Bayshore past Brisbane to Guadalupe Canyon Parkway. Turn left, and travel to the crest where the San Bruno Mountain State and County Park is located. From the north on Highway 101 take the Sierra Point turnoff, and follow Lagoon Rd. to the intersection of Old Bayshore. Turn right at Old Bayshore and proceed north to Guadalupe Canyon Parkway. Turn left, and continue to the park.

Western Access   From the south take I-280 north toward Daly City and take the Mission Street exit. Turn left for one block to San Pedro Road. Turn right on San Pedro Road to Mission Street. After you cross Mission Street San Pedro Road becomes East Market Street. Stay on East Market Street until it becomes Guadalupe Canyon Parkway. Continue east on the Parkway to the crest where the park is located. From the north take I-280 south to John Daly Boulevard. Travel east on John Daly Boulevard to Mission Street. Cross Mission Street where John Daly Boulevard becomes Hillside Boulevard. Stay on Hillside Boulevard until you reach East Market Street. Turn left on East Market Street which shortly becomes Guadalupe Canyon Parkway. Continue east on the Parkway to the crest where the park is located.

Facilities

The only facilities on the mountain proper are located in San Bruno State and County Park. Here you will find picnic tables, restrooms and a telephone. Of course, restaurants and grocery stores are available in both Brisbane and Daly City.

Fees

As of this printing, there is an entrance fee to the park on weekends and holidays. Entrance to the park is free on weekdays.

Weather

Plan on being exposed to wind and cold and then take great delight when you aren't. Fall and spring are beautiful, with only occasional fog and usually warm mornings. Winter is relatively mild much like anywhere else in the Bay Area, but it can turn rainy and cold without warning. Summer days can be treacherous. It is often cold and windy with blowing fog even when the rest of the peninsula is in the eighties.

SAN MATEO COUNTY

Dan Keller

Clapper Rail

THE BAYSHORE

❖

In San Mateo County the Bayshore is paralleled by US Highway 101 (the Bayshore Freeway) for its entire length. At low tide any exit from 101 to the bay can yield good—even outstanding—shore birding in winter. Here and there, a few tiny marshes—the relics of the once-dominant habitat—can yield rails, egrets and dabbling ducks and the newer industrial and office parks are dotted with artificial lagoons supporting their own populations of coots and wintering ducks. By getting off of 101 and following the various frontage roads you can enjoy a satisfactory day of water-oriented birding without ever visiting one of our "hot-spots."

Good land-birding is harder to find. Undeveloped areas and city parks are generally small and cannot offer much in the way of habitat variety. Golf courses can provide good birding but access can be difficult to arrange. On weekends and holidays the courses are crowded and birding is all but impossible without some intrusion on the rights of the golfers.

Birders intent on looking for land species will do best by concentrating their attentions on the areas we've described in the next few pages—particularly Coyote Point, Bayfront Park, Edgewood Park and, to a lesser degree, Foster City.

COYOTE POINT COUNTY PARK

❖

Nick Coiro

Spring ★★★
Summer ★★
Fall ★★★
Winter ★★★★

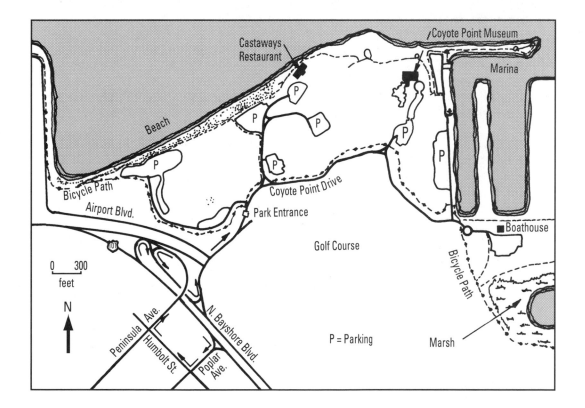

Coyote Point County Recreation Area is situated on San Francisco Bay south of San Francisco Airport and east of the city of San Mateo. From the south you can reach it from either the Dore Avenue or Peninsula Avenue exits of the Bayshore Freeway (US Highway 101).

The park includes a marina and the internationally known Coyote Point Museum for Environmental Education. The Environmental Hall contains exhibits and dioramas depicting the various ecological plant and animal communities of San Mateo County. Each includes a computer game where the visitor can, through various questions, gain a better knowledge of the community. The adjacent wildlife habitat exhibit depicts the various habitats in the county complete with representative live animals. All of the animals are non-releasable, either because they were injured or were pets who became imprinted on humans. There are aviaries for songbirds and raptors. There is a nominal admission charge. It is free on the first Wednesday of the month and is open Tuesday through Sunday. The museum is well worth a visit.

There is also an admission fee to enter the park. On weekdays senior citizens are admitted free. Museum members are admitted free at all times. The fee is seldom collected in the colder months.

In the colder months birding along the bay shore and adjacent marsh can be good for waders and water and shore birds. Land birds are present in the park's wooded and shrubby areas all year, but are more numerous in the winter. The circular tour outlined here can be covered in a morning.

Drive past the entrance station and take the **second left** into the **Museum parking lot**. Park at the lower end near the picnic tables and a rest room building. From there walk straight ahead toward the marina. Go past a corner of the marina and take a paved path leading under some electric transmission towers in a right hand direction. Shortly take a right hand fork downgrade to a small marsh. Check this area for waders, water birds and shorebirds. Also check the trees and towers for raptors. Return to the main path and backtrack to a turnoff to the right bordering the bay and a marsh. Follow the path and go between the marsh and the marina. The "official" path ends at the marina boat entrance. However, a poorly marked and fairly rough trail goes to the right around part of the marsh. This path is difficult to cover in wet weather, but it will get you closer to the birds in the marsh and out on the bay. A California Clapper Rail (an endangered species) was seen and photographed in this marsh in late 1992. (You can purchase note paper featuring this picture in the Museum's gift shop.) If you have a scope scan the breakwater for wintering Surfbirds and turnstones.

Dan Keller

Yellow-rumped Warbler

After covering this area return along the marina and go around it past the Yacht Club building. At the far end (after the divider separating the two sections) turn right and proceed along the other side. While passing the marina look for diving ducks, loons, mergansers and grebes. (A Harlequin Duck was in the bay side of the marina in January 1990). Also look for Belted Kingfishers perched in the boat rigging. Near the Harbormaster's building go left up a path toward the Museum. This path will take you along a bluff above the bay. There are two lookouts with a commanding view of the bay with (on a clear day) San Francisco visible in the distance. Water birds on the bay can be observed from these points. On this path and for the rest of the tour keep checking the trees, bushes and grassy areas for land birds including juncos, Hermit Thrushes, various sparrows, towhees and nuthatches. In winter Yellow-rumped Warblers are here in large numbers.

Continue on this path bearing left (do not take an offshoot to the right toward the Castaways restaurant). Proceed by a path alongside a family picnic area toward a building known as the Captain's House. Go around the house and follow the path back to the starting point. On the pathway beyond the Captain's House be on the lookout for Great Horned Owls that have nested in this area in recent years. Red-tailed Hawks also nested near there in the spring of 1993.

Except for the rough path around the marsh near the marina boat entrance, the whole tour can be done on a bicycle. Restrooms are located in the picnic areas. There is no food service in the park except the Castaways, a fine full service restaurant open for lunch from 11 AM to 2:30 PM. As mentioned above there are many picnic areas. Other restaurants and gas stations are located on Airport Boulevard north of the park entrance toward San Francisco Airport. The San Mateo city golf course is located adjacent to the park and is accessible through the park entrance.

FOSTER CITY

❖

Nick Coiro

Spring ★★★
Summer ★
Fall ★★★★
Winter ★★★★ (Best)

Foster City is situated at the western end of the San Mateo-Hayward Bridge across San Francisco Bay. It is essentially a group of islands with a network of lagoons winding through the city. It is surrounded by Marina Lagoon, Belmont Slough, and San Francisco Bay. Habitat for water birds and shorebirds, including most west coast species, abounds, as well as for marsh and wading birds; this is its chief attraction. Parks, vacant grassy and scrubby areas, plus trees planted throughout the developed areas provide habitat for appropriate species. Raptors patrol much of the shoreline, marshy areas, and fields.

Over 165 species have been observed including such rarities as Tropical Kingbird, Virginia's Warbler, Lesser Nighthawk, Rose-breasted Grosbeak, Eurasian Wigeon, and Tufted Duck. The most famous of these visitors was the Smew which wintered here from 1981 through 1984. Red Knots winter here in fairly large numbers. Hooded Merganser and Barrow's Goldeneye occur each winter. In recent years Peregrine Falcon and Merlin have been found each winter.

The best birding period is October through March when water-oriented birds winter here by the thousands. Birding during the balance of the year is not too productive. Barn and Cliff Swallows are present in good number in the summer. Hooded Orioles are a fairly common nesting species (April–August) in residential areas—check in the vicinity of Fan Palms. Forster's Tern are common along with a few Caspian Terns. Least Terns occur infrequently (in late summer and fall). A few Elegant Terns are present in late summer and early fall.

During the past several years water birds have tended to spread out through the city, where previously they were concentrated in a few spots. While the number of species have not heavily diminished, the total population has shown a noticeable decline. The decline in "puddle ducks" is consistent with national population surveys and is generally believed to be due to the prolonged drought

53

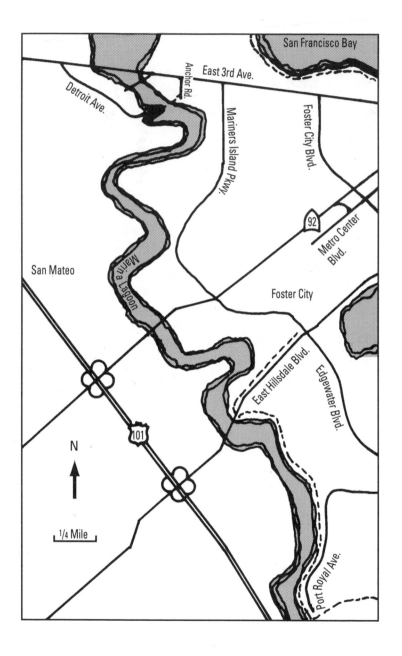

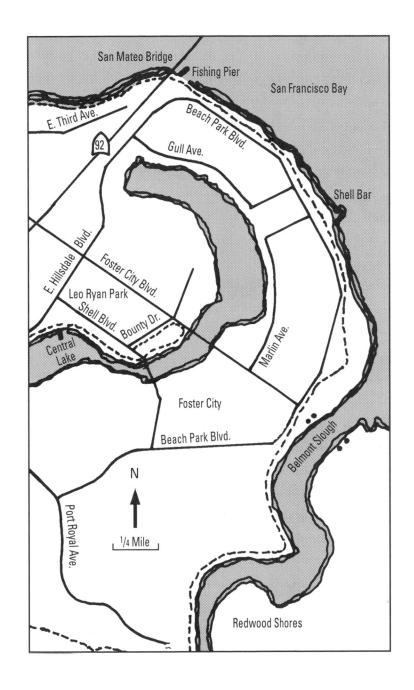

and the loss of much of their nesting habitat on the northern prairies. Both puddle ducks and divers have suffered locally from loss of nearby wetlands. Other factors might be increased human and domestic animal pressure.

❖ **Tip** *You'll find a spotting scope very useful when birding Foster City.*

Directions are provided to each of the birding areas. However, the accompanying map should be consulted for better orientation. Since the birds (particularly water birds) are spread throughout the city, it may be necessary to visit several locations to find your "target" species. Some of the areas are near residences. Residents' privacy must be observed at all times. To cover all of the areas would take most of a day. However, the main areas can be covered in a half day (morning is best).

The Main Foster City Lagoons

Many of the lagoon areas are not readily accessible, but there are enough vantage points to provide observation of water-oriented birds without intruding into people's back yards. Other species can be seen in adjacent grassy and scrubby fields, bridges, and nearby trees and shrubs. Electric transmission towers should be scanned for perching raptors.

Central Lake

Central Lake is located at Leo Ryan Park, on the south side of Hillsdale Boulevard, between Edgewater and Shell Boulevards. You'll find a parking lot on the west side of Shell Boulevard south of the intersection with Hillsdale Boulevard, between the Recreation Center Building and the tennis courts. Park here and walk to the lake. The lake is used by boaters and wind surfers in spring, summer, fall and sometimes on milder winter days, particularly on weekends. Observation is best early to mid-morning and late afternoon. If you'll look to your right as you face the lagoon, you'll see a gazebo built out over the water. This structure provides a good observation point where you won't disturb or be disturbed by the joggers and bikers who use the lakeside paths. It is, however, necessary to move along the shore to observe the entire lagoon.

Wintering birds start arriving in early October, peak in December, and tail off in late January and February. Mallards, coots, and diving ducks are usually present in fairly large numbers. Loons, grebes, mergansers, Brown Pelicans, Double-crested Cormorants, Forster's Terns, and several species of gulls are also present.

Rarities have been observed here, including a Smew (winters of 1981–1984), Common Mergansers, and Red-necked Grebes. Barrow's Goldeneyes and Hooded Mergansers are regular winter visitors.

After birding the lagoon note the *Pyracantha* hedge behind the tiered seating area near the gazebo. Black-crowned Night-Herons, American Robins, Cedar Waxwings, and various sparrows can be found in these bushes and in the nearby trees, particularly when berries are present.

Restroom facilities are available in the Recreation Center buildings as well as in a small building near the gazebo.

When dispersed from the lake, birds can often be found in the canals extending from the lake and behind apartment and condominium buildings. The walkway along the western side of the lagoon is restricted to residents of the apartment complex and is blocked by a fence.

This canal can also be observed from Isle Cove. To get there drive south on Edgewater Boulevard from its intersection with Hillsdale Boulevard about $1/2$ mile and look for a left turn across the boulevard onto Dorado Street and into Isle Cove. Drive onto Dorado and across a small bridge to Andromeda Street, turn right and park in the lot on the left. A walkway extends completely around the island. Many birds that have dispersed from Central Lake can be seen here at close range. Look both north toward Central Lake and south toward a large arched bridge.

An alternative is to drive south on Edgewater Boulevard past Dorado Street to the Edgewater Place Shopping Center at the corner of Edgewater and Beach Park Boulevards. Park and walk onto or under the bridge on Beach Park Boulevard. Many birds can be observed from the bridge.

The walkway on the eastern side of Central Lake passing the tennis courts can also be followed for about a mile passing under a bridge on Shell Boulevard to the bridge on Foster City Boulevard. It is possible to exit at a parking lot on Foster City Boulevard, just before the bridge. From the entrance to the parking lot walk a short distance west to Bounty Drive and continue to the left to Shell Boulevard where a right turn will take you back to Central Lake.

Marina Lagoon

Marina Lagoon extends about 3 miles, from near the intersection of Port Royal Avenue and Rock Harbor Lane at the Lantern Cove housing complex in a generally northern direction to an outlet on San Francisco Bay near East Third Avenue. Birding is possible along most of the lagoon.

Port Royal Avenue can be reached by turning right from Hillsdale Boulevard (when coming from Highway 101) onto Edgewater Boulevard, and proceeding about .8 mile past the Edgewater Place Shopping Center to a right turn on Port Royal Avenue. (*Note that Port Royal is a circular drive and has two intersections with Edgewater. Take the second right onto Port Royal*). Drive to the intersection with Rock Harbor Lane at Lantern Cove and park in the lot to the right. Walk ahead to a paved path leading to the lagoon (toward the freeway). Here, and all along the lagoon, water birds, shorebirds, and waders can be found in fall, winter, and spring. In addition to diving ducks look for dabbling ducks such as Northern Pintail, American Wigeon, Northern Shoveler and Gadwall. Black-bellied Plover, Killdeer, Greater Yellowlegs and Spotted Sandpiper may be present anywhere on the shoreline along the lagoon. Hooded Mergansers and Barrow's Goldeneyes used to congregate in this lagoon but, in recent years, have dispersed to other water areas throughout the city.

A paved path follows the lagoon for almost three miles, passing under three bridges and ends at Shoal Drive and Armada Way. You can walk the entire way. If you have two vehicles, leave one at the Port Royal Avenue-Rock Harbor Lane parking area and the other on Shoal Drive just off of Armada Way This eliminates backtracking. To reach Armada Way, take Edgewater Boulevard (which soon becomes Mariner Island Boulevard) north from its intersection with Hillsdale Boulevard for about a mile and turn left on Armada Way.

Other parts of the lagoon can be observed from various paths along Beach Park Boulevard and Port Royal Avenue. To reach these turn south from Hillsdale Boulevard onto Altair Avenue (first traffic light after entering Foster City from Route 101). At a "Y" turn right onto Polaris Avenue and a little further take a right turn onto Beach Bark Boulevard. Drive slowly along the Boulevard and look for paved paths leading from the right between buildings to the lagoon. Good spots are near the Shell Cove housing development and opposite the intersection with Virgo and Polaris Lanes. When you reach Jamaica Street turn right and shortly turn right again onto Port Royal Avenue. Along Port Royal look for several paths on the right before you arrive at the beginning of the lagoon near the intersection with Rock Harbor Lane.

East Third Avenue Bayshore

East Third Avenue extends from San Mateo east into Foster City. It can be reached from Route 101 by a clearly marked exit. From Foster City it can be reached by traveling north on Edgewater or Foster City Boulevards. from their intersection with Hillsdale Boulevard

Just after crossing Norfolk Street near Ryder Park, about .3 miles from Route 101, you will see a turnoff on the left. Since Third Avenue is a divided road, pass the turnoff, do a legal U-turn and come back to the turnoff.

From the parking area at this turnoff you can take a paved path north along San Francisco Bay about a mile to Coyote Park. It is also possible to walk east along the bay around a closed and landscaped landfill. This path curves back to Third Avenue at the juncture with Detroit Road. These paths can be productive, particularly in the colder months. On all the paths along the bay the main attractions are shorebirds and waders, particularly at low tide. Diving ducks, terns, loons, grebes, and mergansers can be seen further out. Both Surf and White-winged Scoters and usually present and Black Scoters are possible. Oldsquaws have also been seen here.

San Francisco Bay also borders the north side of East Third Avenue from the east end of the paths around the old dump and from a bridge over the mouth of Marina Lagoon for about 1½ miles. A paved path extends along the bay joining a path along another part of Beach Park Boulevard after going under the San Mateo Bridge. If you don't want to hike the entire length of the path you can park in a lot on the bay side of the intersection of East Third Avenue and Anchor Road. From the parking lot scan the PG&E transmission towers for raptors, particularly Peregrine Falcons. Red-tailed Hawks, Accipiters, White-tailed Kites and Common Ravens are often present. One or more Peregrine Falcons have been present every winter for the last several years.

About 250 yards to the right of the parking lot (as you face the Bay) look for a Burrowing Owl among the rocks on an embankment beside the path extending northerly in a semi-circular pattern around another landfill.

Continue east toward the San Mateo Bridge. Beyond the intersection with Foster City Boulevard, you can park off the street or use the parking areas in office complexes. While you are driving along Third Avenue near Foster City Boulevard look toward the Bay and scan the ponds (in wet years) for shorebirds and dabbling ducks. In past years both Red-necked and Red Phalaropes have been present. A Wandering Tattler has been found on the rip-rap along the bayfront in late August and September. Near the San Mateo-Hayward bridge look for Pelagic Cormorants (rare inside the San Francisco Bay) in the water or perched on the underside of the bridge.

Anywhere along the walkway check out the weedy areas for sparrows, Lesser Goldfinches, Pine Siskins, Yellow-rumped Warblers and American Pipits. Kestrels, White-tailed Kites and Loggerhead Shrikes often patrol these fields.

The lower end of Marina Lagoon can be observed by parking on Anchor Road. On the west side of Anchor Road you will find a path leading to Bayside-Joinville Park. Follow the path to a bridge crossing a slough. The lagoon is visible from here. Once again, water-oriented birds are the main attraction.

The San Mateo County Fishing Pier and the Foster City Bayfront Levee

The San Mateo County Fishing Pier offers an excellent opportunity to get closer to the bay ducks, gulls, loons, grebes and cormorants. Brown Pelicans can sometimes be seen roosting here. There is a nesting colony of Double-crested Cormorants on the tall towers alongside the bridge.

The pier is one end of the old San Mateo-Hayward Bridge. Approximately 1500 feet long it is, as its name implies, principally used for fishing, but it is an ideal place for observing the various bay birds. November, December, and January are some of the best months for observing the large number of species which use San Francisco Bay for feeding and resting, including Canvasbacks, both scaups, all three scoters, Ruddy Ducks, Goldeneyes, Buffleheads, loons, and grebes. It should be noted that in recent years Clark's Grebes have outnumbered Western Grebes in Foster City.

You can get there by going east on Hillsdale Boulevard from Bayshore Highway (Route 101) approximately 2½ miles. The entrance to the fishing pier parking lot is about .2 miles beyond the stop sign at Gull Avenue (the Port of Call Shopping Center is at this intersection) and directly opposite Teal Avenue.

The levee runs along the bay south of the fishing pier. From the path along the levee you can see larger shorebirds roosting at high tide and both large and small shorebirds feeding at low tide. About a mile south of the bridge (near the Beach Park Shopping Center) you'll find a large spit extending into the bay. This spit is composed of clam and mussel shells and so it is locally known as the shell bar. At high tide (the best viewing is just before and after the peak of the tide) from September through April you can see thousands of shorebirds resting here. Some are present all year. This is the best spot to see Red Knots, (which will be in basic (winter) plumage without a trace of red). Willets, Dowitchers, Marbled

Godwits, Dunlins, Western and Least Sandpipers, Whimbrels, Long-billed Curlews, Black-bellied and Semipalmated Plovers and Black and Ruddy Turnstones also use the shell bar as a resting place. Gulls and Terns share the spit with them. In late summer and early fall look for Elegant Terns. At all times be alert for raptors, particularly Merlins and Harriers surveying the shorebird flocks.

Belmont Slough

Belmont Slough extends from San Francisco Bay near the intersection of Halibut Street and Beach Park Boulevard toward Marina Lagoon. A narrow canal connects Belmont Slough and Marina Lagoon. A paved path extends along these waterways all the way to Marina Lagoon. A marshy area of varying width lies between the path and the slough.

Great Blue Herons and Black-crowned Night-Herons, as well as Great and Snowy Egrets, shorebirds and waterfowl all feed here. Further along the slough you will come to a cemented intake. Eurasian Wigeons can often be found here in winter and Green-winged and Cinnamon Teal in spring. Barn Swallows have nested under the intake in summer. A large flooded pond on the right a short way further along the slough hosts many shorebirds. These are mostly larger species (American Avocet, Black-necked Stilt, Long-billed Curlew, Whimbrel, dowitchers, and Willets) resting on the small islands in the pond. Several species of gulls and a variety of dabbling ducks are also usually present. Caspian Terns also use this as a rest area in summer. A walk around the pond, sometimes to see the birds in better light, can be rewarding. While taking this walk, view the lagoon to the west of the pond for more water birds, including grebes, loons, merganser, and Brown Pelicans. A Tufted Duck was in the lagoon in February 1993.

Waterfowl and shorebirds predominate in or near the slough, as you progress to its end. Keep looking for Song and Savannah Sparrows in the marsh and grassy areas. American Kestrels, Merlins, White-tailed Kites, Red-tailed Hawks, Northern Harriers and Turkey Vultures may perch on the transmission towers near the slough. In some years Short-eared Owls have also been seen over the marshy areas. Particularly check the PG&E transmission towers across the slough near the intersections of Beach Park and Foster City Boulevard's for Peregrine Falcons. Check the overhead wires for perching White-tailed Kites.

If you want to walk the entire length of the slough, park on Beach Park Boulevard (Bayside) north of Foster City Boulevard. Be careful that you are not in the red-curbed no parking zone. If you have two vehicles you can park one here and the other in the parking area near Lantern Cove (described in the section on Marina Lagoon) and therefore avoid backtracking.

Parts of the Slough can be viewed from the side streets. From Hillsdale Boulevard follow Edgewater Boulevard south to its end (about 2 miles) at Balfour Street. Drive straight into the Schooner Bay Development and take the right-hand fork and park where you can. Walk forward to the slough. While here also walk into Quadrant Lane (on the right) to a series of ponds around some residence buildings. In winter these ponds are usually filled with dabbling ducks, particularly American Wigeons, and Canada Geese. At the time this was written this is the best area in the city to see Eurasian Wigeons. One or several have wintered here for the last few years. Also look for Common Snipe on the lawns.

After viewing this area return to Balfour and turn right. Go approximately .2 mile, turn right and then left into the parking area. From here you can park and walk to the Slough. Both viewing areas are good for Green-winged and Cinnamon Teal and sometimes for Hooded Merganser and Barrow's Goldeneye. The Eurasian race of the Green-winged Teal has been seen in the slough in this general area. Scan the electric transmission towers here for a Merlin. In late 1992 a Golden Eagle used these towers for several weeks.

Other Lagoon Areas

With the dispersal of water birds through Foster City in recent years it may be necessary to visit several areas to see most of the species. Several other lagoon areas can be very productive and contain several species of water fowl.

San Miguel Lane

While proceeding south along Edgewater Boulevard turn left on Pitcairn Drive. Follow it to San Miguel Lane (about ½ mile) and park at a levee near open water. You'll find Mergansers, Hooded and Red-breasted, and Goldeneye, both Common and Barrow's, as well as other waterfowl. To the right of Pitcairn Drive is Sea Cloud Park. The park is used heavily, particularly on weekends. However, land birds including pipits, meadowlarks, sparrows, blackbirds and occasionally a flicker can be found in the grassy areas and trees. Most importantly, there are restrooms at the park.

Corsica Lane

After checking these areas back-track on Pitcairn Drive to Corsica Lane. Turn right and proceed to an intersection with Trinidad Lane. Park near the intersection and walk forward between the buildings to an open lagoon. Many water birds like those mentioned above can be found here.

Ponds on Port Royal Avenue

Return to Edgewater Boulevard and continue south past the Edgewater Place Shopping Center. Turn right at the second intersection with Port Royal Avenue. In a short time you will see several ponds on the left in front of some residences. These ponds are sometimes full of dabbling ducks and gulls. Eurasian Wigeons have been here in recent winters but were absent in 1992-1993. The area is worth a brief check.

Port-of-Call Shopping Center

The open lagoon behind the Port of Call Shopping Center can be productive. The center is located on Hillsdale Boulevard at its intersection with Gull Avenue. From Hillsdale Boulevard (when traveling toward the Bay) enter the shopping center just before the intersection and proceed to a parking area on the far right. View the open lagoon from this spot for concentrations of waterfowl. This area can be visited in connection with a visit to the Fishing Pier.

Birding Foster City By Bicycle

In the text above many references were made to paved paths along the levees and lagoons. Using these it is possible to bicycle (or walk) completely around Foster City. Bicycling allows you to cover a greater area and thus see more birds. Participants on one recent bike trip were able to identify 75 species. If you're coming from out of town it's best to park in the Fishing Pier parking lot and start with the bike path along the Bay. You can go either left or right. Left is best at low tide and right at high tide. The path covers about 11 miles and extends along the Bay Front levee, Belmont Slough, Marina Lagoon, and the bayshore along East Third Avenue. If you have traveled from the right it will be necessary to leave the bike path just before going under the third bridge over Marina Lagoon (about 6 miles from the starting point) and take a right along Fashion Island Boulevard to Mariner's Island Boulevard. Turn left and bike along Mariner's Island Boulevard (in the bike lane) to its intersection with East Third Avenue. Cross Third Avenue and enter the bike path running along the Bay. At this point you can go either left or right - left toward the old landfill and Coyote Point or right along the Bay back to the Fishing Pier parking lot. Before proceeding along Third Avenue check the transmission tower for raptors, particularly Peregrine Falcon. These bike paths are very popular and heavily used on weekends and holidays. Sequoia Audubon has conducted a popular field trip around the city on bikes for the last few years. Plan on taking a full morning to cover the entire bike path.

Directions

Foster City can be reached by traveling east from the Bayshore Freeway (Highway 101) at the Hillsdale, Highway 92 or Third Avenue exits. From the East Bay it can be reached via the San Mateo-Hayward Bridge (Highway 92) exiting at Foster City Boulevard or Edgewater Boulevard South. Public transportation is available but a car or bicycle is needed to cover a variety of areas.

Facilities

There are plenty of places to eat in Foster City, ranging from delicatessens and fast food to large dinner restaurants. Service stations are easy to find, but only on the main streets. Several shopping centers of varying sizes dot the city with their grocery stores, drugstores, and specialty shops. If you're in dire need of a major shopping center, the large Hillsdale Mall is located in San Mateo about a mile west of Foster City on Hillsdale Boulevard. It has department stores, specialty shops, and restaurants. Restrooms can be found in Sea Cloud Park, Leo Ryan Park, gas stations and restaurants.

Nearby points of interest

Sequoia Audubon Society's office is nearby, just south of Hillsdale Mall off El Camino Real at 30 West 39th Avenue. Checklists of Foster City are available at the office or by mail. Redwood Shores, another good birding area, is nearby. Its description follows this section.

Possible changes

The city is raising the levees along the bayshore and the sloughs as a flood control measure. At this time the extent of the change does not appear to be likely to have an effect on the wildlife viewing or the use of the various paths and trails.

Dan Keller

Barrow's Goldeneye

REDWOOD SHORES

❖

Nick Coiro

Spring ★★★
Summer ★
Fall ★★★
Winter ★★★★

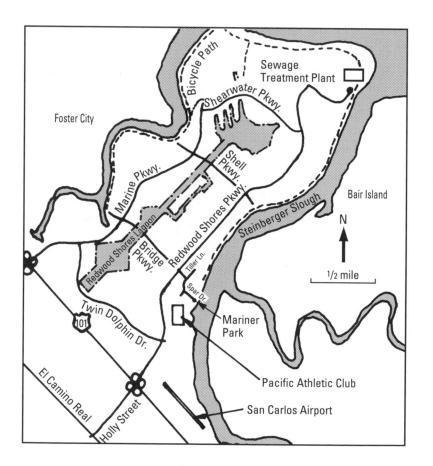

Redwood Shores is a residential community that is part of Redwood City even though it is physically isolated from it and is nearer Belmont and San Carlos. It has been developed extensively in recent years. Nevertheless, some good birding areas exist and should remain. Water oriented birds, waterfowl, waders, and shorebirds are the chief attraction. However land birds and raptors are present and should be looked for along water areas and grassy and shrubby areas and trees. Some notable birds have been found including, Hooded Mergansers, Barrow's Goldeneye, Blue-winged Teal, a Eurasian Green-winged Teal, Eurasian Wigeons, and Peregrine Falcons. Short-eared Owls, once regular here, have been impacted by development but may still be seen over the marshes and fields near Belmont Slough (a few pairs nest on nearby Bair Island).

Several areas will be mentioned below along with directions. They can be visited separately. However, making a somewhat circular tour of the community in order see a variety of birds is probably best. Such a tour is described below.

Birding here is best from September through April with the largest concentrations in November-March. Summer months are not very productive.

To begin the tour enter Redwood Shores from the Bayshore Highway (Route 101) by taking the Holly Street/Redwood Shores Parkway exit east. Drive past the Pacific Athletic Club (large building on the right) and park on the left side of the parking lot. Walk forward to view a large pond behind a fence. This pond usually contains a good variety of dabbling and diving ducks plus shorebirds, gulls, and waders. Eurasian Wigeons, Blue-winged Teal (rare), and both the American and Eurasian Green-winged Teal are sometimes present in this pond. The grassy areas here and along this route are currently the best places in the county to find Horned Larks. You will find exotic, domestic and Canada Geese here (and throughout the Redwood Shores area) year-round.

After viewing this area continue on Redwood Shores Parkway to Bridge Parkway. Turn right and then right again on Tiller Lane at the sign for Mariner Park. Take Tiller Lane to its end and turn left on Spar Drive. Continue to a circular ending and park. Walk to a levee overlooking Steinberger Slough. At low tide many shore birds will be present. Waterfowl can also be present in the slough at anytime. A levee path runs along the slough in both directions. To the right there is a fence blocking the path. It is now possible to go through the fence but this policy seems to change on a day-to-day basis. On the other side is another view of the pond mentioned above. On sunny mornings this is the best vantage point as it keeps the sun at your back. It also gives you a chance to scan the opposite shore and the areas concealed by the small islands in the center.

Return to Redwood Shores Parkway and continue along it for a short distance. Turn left on Cringle Drive. Park at the intersection of Cringle and Neptune at Marlin Park and check out part of the Belmont Channel for dabbling and diving ducks. There should be many song birds among the bushes along the channel to the right. If time permits check out the channel beyond the open field on the right along Davit Lane for more water birds. Coots are often found on the lawns.

Return again to Redwood Shores Parkway and continue along for about 0.2 mile past Shell Parkway and turn right on Avocet Drive. A large water tank will be on the right. Turn right on the access road immediately past the water tank and park at the end of the road (about 100 yards from the turnoff). There is a dirt path along Steinberger Slough where a marsh and open water can be observed for appropriate birds.

Return one more time to the parkway and continue about 0.9 mile (past Shearwater Parkway) to a radio station building. In wet weather stop here to survey the field for small shorebirds. American Pipits and Horned Larks can also be present at any time. The road turns to the right. Continue along it to the entrance to a sewage plant installation. Park near the entrance and walk to the right to the path along Steinberger Slough. Check out the slough for water and shorebirds and the marsh areas on the left for dabbling ducks, sparrows, Yellow-rumped Warblers, House Finches, Black Phoebes and Marsh Wrens. If time permits walk along the path toward the bay past some ponds on the left and circle the sewage plant. The endangered California Clapper Rail has nested in the marshy areas near the plant and has been seen crossing the levee to feed along the slough. Snowy and Great Egrets, driven from their normal nesting areas on nearby Bair Island by the invasive, introduced red fox have established a rookery and roost in the small trees near this marsh. With Black-crowned Night-Herons—the previous tenants—continuing to nest in the trees, the rookery is over-crowded. Do not approach too closely during nesting season. These birds have enough problems already without our adding to them. The trees themselves are beginning to break down because of the combined weight of the birds and the over-fertilization of the soil from bird droppings. If you're here during the nesting season check the electric transmission towers across the slough for nesting Double-crested Cormorants and Great Blue Herons.

Look for raptors on electric transmission towers and the radio antennae. Sometimes a Peregrine Falcon can be found in this area. Common Ravens have built a nest on these towers in recent years.

After viewing this area backtrack on Redwood Shores Parkway to Shell Parkway. Turn right. Continue on Shell to its end at a cul-de-sac. There is a marshy area and open water—a part of Belmont Slough—at this location. Check this area for the appropriate waterfowl and shorebirds. There is an unpaved path running both to the left and right. Look for Horned Larks (has nested) and American Pipit (spring and winter) in the nearby fields.

Return on Shell Parkway to Marine Parkway (in some places this street's name is still identified as Marine World Parkway, reminding us that the theme park was once located here) and turn right. Continue to Bridge Parkway and take another right turn. Park at the end where you can walk forward to a lower part of Belmont Slough. Here it is possible to view parts of this slough difficult to check out from Foster City. There is an unpaved path going toward the Bay for a considerable distance with fields and seasonal ponds. Shorebirds and dabbling ducks can be found in the ponds and Horned Larks and American Pipits can be found here as well.

A little further along Marine Parkway look for Marine Park Center on the left. Turn left across the Parkway and park. This center is private property and should be respected as such. Forward and to the right is an extension of the Belmont Channel. The area is heavily populated with domestic geese and ducks. However, it should be checked for wintering bay ducks, loons, grebes, and mergansers. Both Barrow's Goldeneye's and Hooded Mergansers are frequently present at this season. This fairly well completes the somewhat circular tour and Marine Parkway can be followed a little further to an exit on the Bayshore Freeway (Route 101).

The tour can be completed in a full morning if time is not spent on extended walks along the levees. If time is short it is recommended that birding be limited to the fenced in pond near the Pacific Athletic Club, the marsh and open water at Avocet Drive, the sewage plant marsh and Marine Park Center. A good variety of birds can be found at these areas with a good chance to find the more sought-after species.

❖ **Note** *There is currently much new development in this area and by the time of publication, we expect some locations described here to be covered with buildings.*

Birding Redwood Shores by Bicycle

A trail (mostly unpaved) almost completely encircles Redwood Shores. Using this trail it is possible to observe most of the water areas and undeveloped land areas by bicycle (or on foot). As with Foster City, this will permit a more complete coverage of Redwood Shores and you have the potential for observing more birds and more species. Most of the bird life will be water and shore birds; however since you will be covering a lot of undeveloped land other appropriate species can be found. Be alert for hawks and Short-eared Owls over the marsh and undeveloped grassy areas.

The path is mostly unpaved and can be almost impassable in wet weather. It is fairly rough and rutted in some areas. A mountain bike is most suitable but the writer has covered it often on a regular bike.

To take the tour drive into Redwood Shores via Marine Parkway (Ralston exit on Route 101). Park in the large Oracle Building Parking lot on Oracle Parkway (left turn from Marine Parkway) and go to a paved path across the road. Move to the right around a slough extension and proceed along Belmont Slough toward the bay. Border the slough all the way to the Sewage Plant. Even though the path may narrow at times, it is passable for its entire length. Continue from there along Steinberger Slough until you reach the fence near the pond by the Athletic Club referred to earlier. Exit the path here and ride along Spar Drive, turning right on Tiller Lane. At Bridge Parkway turn left and take it to its end just beyond Marine Parkway. At the end of Bridge Parkway go up an embankment back onto the trail; turn left and retrace your path to the starting area. The entire tour, about eight miles, will take a half day.

Bridge Parkway can also be your starting point. The large paved circle at the end of the parkway is a good place to park and gain access to the path. At this time there are few stores and no gas stations in Redwood Shores. Restrooms and picnic areas are available at Marlin Park and along Marine Parkway at Shorebird Park. There is a gas station at the entrance to Redwood Shores near Marine (World) Parkway. Other gas stations and restaurants are located along El Camino Real in San Carlos. To reach them just continue west past Highway 101 to El Camino. Plans have been advanced to raise the levees along the sloughs as a flood control measure. The final extent of this change and its possible effects on wildlife viewing and use of the levees is unknown.

Mary Molteni

Gadwall

BAYFRONT PARK

❖

Robin Smith and Dan Keller

Spring ★★★
Summer ★
Fall ★★
Winter ★★

Bayfront Park is located in Menlo Park just north and west of the Dumbarton Bridge. The center hilly area is bounded on two sides by tidal marsh and on the other two by salt ponds. The results of creative land use are visible here. The hilly area was once a fill-and-cover refuse disposal area (dump).

Visit at low tide to see the most species. A level trail circles the outer reaches of the area and several other trails undulate through the central hills. This is a good place for a stroll at dusk on hot summer days to enjoy the cooling bay winds.

After entering the gates at the intersection of Marsh Road and Bayfront Expressway, park on the right and check the slough and marsh on the left as well as the diked tidal marsh on the right, for herons, egrets, ducks, gulls, terns and shorebirds. There are two paved parking lots farther along this road. Trails that lead into the park start from these parking areas. Plan to spend a couple of hours on foot—this will allow time to cover the various habitats. Enjoy the view of the bay from the hilltops—keep an eye out for raptors overhead and land birds in the grass at your feet. Scan the fence posts for American Kestrels, Say's Phoebe, Western Meadowlark and sparrows. Look for Ring-necked Pheasants and Jackrabbits on the slopes. Thank former Menlo Park City Manager Mike Bedwell for having the foresight to turn the local midden into a park.

Birds to Look For

Common Year-Round Residents
Double-crested Cormorant, Gadwall, Turkey Vulture, American Kestrel, Northern Harrier, Red-tailed Hawk, Forster's Tern, Rock Dove, Mourning Dove, European Starling, Ring-necked Pheasant (introduced), Anna's Hummingbird,

Song Sparrow, Savannah Sparrow, Mallard, Great Blue Heron, Great Egret, Snowy Egret, American Avocet, Black-necked Stilt, Black Phoebe, Northern Mockingbird, Common Raven, Western Meadowlark, Red-winged and Brewer's Blackbirds, and House Finch.

Winter Visitors
White-tailed Kite, Least and Western Sandpipers, Dunlin, Dowitchers, Willet, Whimbrel, Long-billed Curlew, Marbled Godwit, Greater Yellowlegs, Killdeer, Western and Clark's Grebe, Pied-billed Grebe, Northern Shoveler, Canvasback, Bufflehead, Bonaparte's and Western Gulls, Loggerhead Shrike, Say's Phoebe, American Pipit, Yellow-rumped Warbler, Golden-crowned Sparrow, and White-crowned Sparrow.

Common Spring and Summer Visitors
Violet-green, Barn and Cliff Swallows and American Goldfinch.

Infrequent Visitors
Peregrine Falcon, Caspian Tern, Black-bellied Plover, Canada Goose, Northern Pintail, Common Goldeneye, American Wigeon, Green-winged Teal, Blue-winged Teal, Cinnamon Teal, Ruddy Duck, Greater and Lesser Scaup, Western Kingbird and Horned Lark. Lapland Longspurs were found here on at least two occasions in winter.

Directions

Take US 101 to Marsh Road. Exit east toward the bay. At the stoplight continue through the intersection and enter Bayfront Park. Open year round from dawn to dusk. Bathroom facilities are available at 1st parking area. Bring water and your dog on a leash. For sustenance head to downtown Menlo Park. [*Note: SamTrans says you can get close on the 51B bus from the Redwood City Caltrain Station*]

EDGEWOOD COUNTY PARK

❖

*Wilma Rockman Updated by Rick Johnson
with help from Toni Corelli (Native Plants)*

Spring ★★★★
Summer ★★
Fall ★★
Winter ★★★

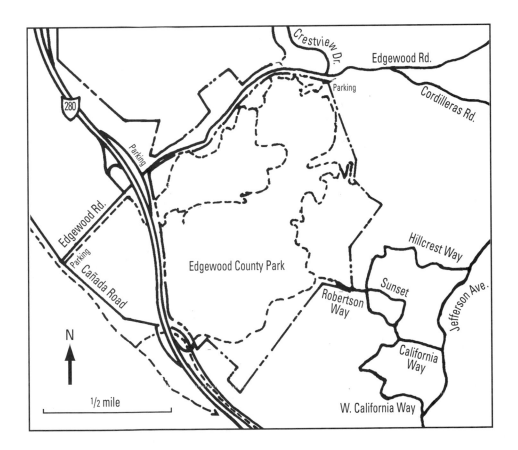

Edgewood County Park contains a rich sampling of three major habitats: oak woodland, chaparral, and grassland. Approximately 70 species of birds are found here, including migrants and residents. The greatest number of species (45–60) at varying seasons can be found in the oak woodland habitat; 20–30 species can be found in the other major habitats. More than 300 species of plants have been identified within the park. Of interest to botanists are a variety of rare plants: San Mateo Thornmint, Marin Dwarf Flax, Fragrant Fritillary, San Francisco Collinsia, Western Leatherwood and White-rayed Pentacheata. The park contains 110 acres of serpentine soil which support a grassland rich in native and endemic species. The grasslands have rich insect populations and are a breeding site for Grasshopper Sparrows and Western Meadowlarks. Water sources include minor wetlands with permanent springs and seeps. Seasonal runoffs provide streams in the winter and spring. As an introduction to birding in this area, you should follow the approximately two mile trail around the ridge that forms the park's center. This ridge stands out like a tree-capped island with its shores buried in waves of grasslands. The habitat found on the ridge is primarily oak woodland on the north side and top, and chaparral on the south side. The views of San Francisco Bay and Crystal Springs Lake from the trails are spectacular. With few exceptions, all of the trails have a 10% gradient. Avoid using closed trails made many years ago by motorcycles and off-road vehicles since these areas are still regenerating. Don't add to erosion!

Some of the flora found on the ridge are:

- Trees: Pacific Madrone, Valley Oak, Live Oak, Silk Tassel, Scrub Oak, Buckeye, California Bay

- Understory: Poison Oak(!!!), Coffee Berry, Honeysuckle, Toyon, bedstraw, snowberry

- Chaparral: Chamise, Coyote Brush, monkeyflower, Pitcher Sage, *Ceanothus*, California Broom

- Grasses: brome grass, *stipa*, California Oatgrass, Squirreltail, quaking grass

- Other: ferns, lichens, mosses, fungi

Viewed from the ridge from March to May, the grasslands below provide an annual display of spring flowers of exceptional beauty. Allow two to three hours for one of the loop trails.

Birds to look for

Year-round species
Turkey Vulture, Cooper's, Red-tailed and Red-shouldered Hawks, American Kestrel, Golden Eagle (rare), California Quail, Band-tailed Pigeon, Mourning Dove, Rock Dove, Anna's Hummingbird, Northern Flicker, Downy, Hairy and Nuttall's Woodpeckers, Black Phoebe, Scrub and Steller's Jays, Common Raven, American Crow, Chestnut-backed Chickadee, Plain Titmouse, White-breasted Nuthatch, Bushtit, Brown Creeper, Wrentit, Bewick's Wren, Northern Mockingbird, California Thrasher, American Robin, Western Bluebird, European Starling, Hutton's Vireo, Western Meadowlark, Brewer's Blackbird, California and Rufous-sided Towhees, Dark-eyed Junco, Song and Savannah Sparrows, Purple and House Finches, Pine Siskin, Lesser and American Goldfinches and House Sparrow.

Spring and summer species
Allen's Hummingbird, Olive-sided, Pacific-slope and Ash throated Flycatchers, Western Wood-Pewee, Violet-green, Tree, Barn, Cliff and Northern Rough-winged Swallows, Swainson's Thrush, Blue-gray Gnatcatcher, Orange-crowned and Wilson's Warblers, Brown-headed Cowbird, Northern Oriole, Black-headed Grosbeak, Chipping and Grasshopper Sparrows.

Winter species
White-tailed Kite, Sharp-shinned Hawk, Northern Harrier, Say's Phoebe, Hermit and Varied Thrushes, Ruby-crowned and Golden-crowned Kinglets, Yellow-rumped and Townsend's Warblers, Golden-crowned, White-crowned and Fox Sparrows.

Directions

There are three entrances to the park: Sunset Way; Edgewood Road west of Interstate 280; and the Old Stage Day Camp entrance on the south side of Edgewood Road adjacent to Crestview Drive. The best entrance to the ridge trail is at the junction of Sunset Way and Hillcrest Way. Take Jefferson Avenue west from El Camino Real in Redwood City. Watch for Jefferson to turn right sharply at Farm Hill Boulevard. After making the turn, proceed about 1.8 miles and turn right on California Way. (Look for the firehouse on the corner). Park at the junction of Sunset Way and Hillcrest Way. Walk past the PG&E substation to the

Dan Keller

Blue-gray Gnatcatcher

locked service road gate. The entrance is adjacent to the gate. Follow the service road to the right, where San Francisco Bay can be seen. The trail starts on the left. Other access points are marked on the map.

Facilities

The only restrooms and picnic facilities are at the Old Stage Day Camp entrance to Edgewood County Park.

Publications

Those interested in the relationship of plants and birds as an aid to identification may wish to read American Wildlife and Plants (A Guide to Wildlife Food Habits) by Martin, Zim and Nelson (Dover Paperback), or the section on food and feeding habits in the Audubon Society Encyclopedia of North American Birds by John K. Terres (Alfred A. Knopf). Recommended publications on plants of the area are Native Shrubs of the San Francisco Bay Region by Roxanna Ferris and Native Trees of the San Francisco Bay Region by Woodbridge Metcalf (both University of California Press paperbacks).

Nearby Areas

Pulgas Ridge Preserve north of Edgewood Park and across Edgewood Road is managed by the Midpeninsula Open Space District. Pulgas Ridge has a nice loop trail (400' elevation gain) through oak woodlands and chaparral. Enter the Preserve along a trail that begins on Edmunds Road off of Crestview. Look for Blue-gray Gnatcatchers in spring along the ridge.

The Interstate 280 overpass where 280 crosses Edgewood Road has a number of cavities that are used for nesting. In May and June look under the bridge for breeding Rough-winged Swallows, and, sometimes, White-throated Swifts.

THE MID-PENINSULA

❖

The Peninsula is a northern extension of the Santa Cruz Mountains. To the north erosion has shaped these mountains into lower and more rounded shapes as exemplified by San Francisco's notorious hills.

The peaks of these ridges and mountains form the spine of the Peninsula. Skyline Drive (California Highway 35) begins in San Francisco and follows these peaks for the length of San Mateo County. On its course it undergoes a number of metamorphoses and name changes. Sometimes it parallels Interstate 280 (The Junipero Serra Freeway), sometimes it is I-280 and for a short stretch it shares State Highway 92. In some cities it is known as Skyline Highway and elsewhere it is Skyline Boulevard.

Along most of its length it lies slightly east of the actual hilltops and you will be treated to spectacular views of the Bay. For a short distance south of its intersection with Highway 92 there are equally spectacular views of the Pacific as well.

Even in its most urbanized

Rufous-sided Towhee

northern areas you can regularly find Kestrels and Red-tailed Hawks perched on utility poles. As you proceed south, you will soon find Turkey Vultures and Northern Harriers working the open spaces on both sides of the road.

In general, the birding improves as you move south out of the more urbanized areas, but even in its most northern areas Skyline Drive can offer some unique birding opportunities.

SWEENEY RIDGE

❖

The Eastern Access—San Bruno
Cliff Richer Updated by Carol Miller

Spring ★★★
Summer ★
Fall ★★★
Winter ★★★

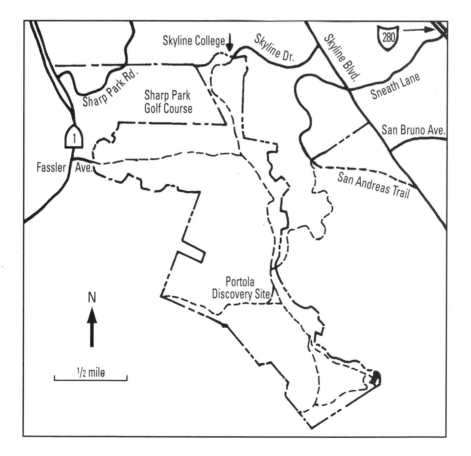

The principal eastern access to Sweeney Ridge begins at the end of Sneath Lane in San Bruno. From either El Camino Real, Skyline Boulevard in San Bruno, or Interstate 280 take Sneath Lane west to where it ends at a locked gate. There is parking space for a small number of vehicles in a small paved parking lot. The road is narrow at this point and if you have a larger vehicle, such as a mobile home, you may find it difficult to turn around.

The area beyond the gate is part of the San Francisco Watershed and public access was previously prohibited. In late spring of 1984 the prohibition was lifted to the extent of allowing foot traffic along the paved road that leads to the top of Sweeney Ridge and the Portola Discovery Site.

This area is a good example of relatively undisturbed coastal chaparral habitat. The paved road winds its way at a relatively easy grade approximately 1.5 miles. There is one moderately steep but short stretch. On a clear day the views of the San Francisco Bay and the peninsula are spectacular, with the panorama stretching from the outskirts of San Jose in the south to Mt. Diablo to the east. These views alone are well worth the climb. From the top of the ridge, you can look out over the ocean to the Farallon Islands, Point Reyes, and Mount Tamalpais to the northwest. A barbed wire fence parallels the road for most of its length, defining the limits of public access. But the density of the chaparral and the presence of poison oak form a more formidable barrier to all but the most dedicated or foolhardy trespasser. The area is managed as a wildlife refuge by the state Department of Fish and Game and deer, skunks and raccoons are abundant.

The bird life is typical of coast chaparral. Wrentits, Bushtits, California Towhees and White-crowned Sparrows are abundant at all seasons. Anna's and Allen's Hummingbirds, Red-tailed Hawks, Wilson's Warblers, Bewick's Wrens, Song Sparrows, Rufous-sided Towhees, Scrub Jays, Band-tailed Pigeons, American and Lesser Goldfinches, House Finches, Turkey Vultures and California Quail have been identified as nesting species. Common Yellowthroats nest in the marshy area at the beginning of the trail, and Black-headed Grosbeaks can be heard singing in the spring.

Those who are unfamiliar with our coastal climate should be warned to expect as much as a 20 degree difference in temperature between the sheltered areas near the gate and the ridge top, particularly when fog is rolling in. There is also a coastal access to this site. For more details on the site and its historical significance, see the Sweeney Ridge description under the Coastal section of this book.

Directions

From El Camino Real (Hwy. 82), (Approx. three miles), Interstate 280 (two miles) or Skyline Boulevard (one mile.) in San Bruno, take Sneath Lane west to where it ends in a small paved parking lot with a locked gate. You may note an isolated and forbidding-looking building to the right as you proceed on Sneath Lane. This is the San Francisco City Jail, about eight miles south of the San Francisco city limits.

Facilities

There are no facilities on Sweeney Ridge itself. Gas stations and restaurants can be found along Skyline Drive or El Camino Real in San Bruno.

Skyline College

If you have a few minutes to spare you may want to backtrack a short distance to check the grounds of Skyline College. To get there return to Skyline Drive and drive north one block to the next set of traffic lights. Turn left (west) and follow the road to the vista point at the furthest western end of the campus. This provides a view of Pacifica and the grassy hillsides below. South of the campus there are a number of student parking lots surrounded by conifers. These can be worth a quick look. Early in the morning you can sometimes find Canada Geese grazing on the lawns.

SAN FRANCISCO WATERSHED

❖

Mary Bresler and Judy Spitler
with special contributions by Peter J. Metropulos and Rick Johnson

Spring ★★★   Fall ★★
Summer ★★   Winter ★★★

The watershed consists of three large man-made lakes and their surrounding hills. The **San Andreas, Upper** and **Lower Crystal Springs Reservoirs** are located in a 15 mile linear valley owned by the City and County of San Francisco for the purpose of maintaining a water supply for its citizens.

In its early years, water was one of the greatest needs of the city. The lack of water was both dangerous (San Francisco burned to the ground six times because there was no water to put out fires) and expensive (costing as much as a dollar a bucketful).

In 1858 the Spring Valley Water Works was founded in San Francisco in an attempt to meet the growing water needs of the city. They hired a young German engineer, Herman Schussler, who built the San Andreas Dam in 1868 . The Sawyer Camp trail crosses this dam. Ten years later, he constructed the Upper Crystal Springs Dam, now the Highway 92 causeway between Upper and Lower Crystal Springs Reservoirs. His greatest engineering feat, however, was the building of what was then the world's largest concrete dam, the Crystal Springs Dam across San Mateo Creek. It was completed in 1890 and visited by engineers from all over the world. It is located on Skyline Drive (Highway 35), just south of Crystal Springs Road. The dam withstood the 1906 earthquake, even though pipes that lay only a few hundred feet away were sheared off.

This valley lies along the infamous San Andreas fault, the area of fracture between two of the earth's major plates. The Pacific Plate is on the west and the American Plate on the east. As you walk along the Sawyer Camp Trail you parallel this fault zone, and you walk mostly on the American Plate.

The entire watershed area is maintained as a wildlife refuge and most of the area is inaccessible to the public. Over the years this policy has become more liberal and may be subject to change in the future. At this time however we will have to settle for viewing the lakes from the eastern boundary. Fortunately, the boundary area is itself rich in beauty, history and birds.

The northernmost reservoir is **San Andreas Lake**. A trail extends along it from San Bruno Avenue south to Hillcrest Boulevard where it connects to the the Sawyer Camp Trail. The first two miles is paved, but the southern .7 mile is gravel and not passable by bicycles which have to detour to the frontage road to get to the Sawyer Camp Trail. As you walk down the trail from the north entrance, you can see in the west the point on Sweeney Ridge from which Gaspar de Portola first saw San Francisco Bay in 1769. You will have lovely views of San Andreas Lake and the wooded mountains beyond as you walk through groves of Monterey Pine and old cypress and open grassy areas. Unfortunately, most of the trail parallels Interstate 280 and the resulting traffic noise intrudes on birding by ear. The birds are similar to those listed below for the Sawyer Camp Trail, but pay particular attention to the transmission towers along the way for they are often used by raptors, which may include a rare Merlin and Peregrine Falcon, especially in the winter.

Sawyer Camp Trail is a beautiful 6.5 mile paved multi-use trail extending from Hillcrest Boulevard south to Crystal Springs Road. It gets extremely heavy use, particularly on the weekends. Watch for bicyclists. (The county has had to impose a bicycle speed limit as there have been a number of injuries from collisions with walkers, runners and other bicycles.)

This land was owned by Leander Sawyer around 1853 and the trail was the access to his camp. Later it was used by the stage coach to Half Moon Bay. The trail is generally downhill going south, particularly in the first mile or so until you reach San Andreas Dam.

In winter be sure to scan the reservoir from the overlook 100 yards north of the dam. Such county rarities as Wood Ducks, Hooded and Common Mergansers and Ospreys have been spotted from here. On at least one occasion, a Red-necked Grebe was found.

This area from the dam to the north end of Lower Crystal Springs Reservoir is the most productive for birds. Moist woods (willow, live oak, bay and buckeye) along the stream are alive with singing birds and wildflowers from March through July. Look for California Quail, Band-tailed Pigeons, Downy, Hairy and Acorn Woodpeckers, California Thrashers, Brown Creepers, Winter and Bewick's Wrens, Hutton's Vireos and Purple Finches year-round. Allen's Hummingbirds, Pacific-slope Flycatchers, Western Wood-Pewees, Warbling Vireos, Wilson's and Orange-crowned Warblers and Black-headed Grosbeaks are common in summer. Hermit Thrushes, Golden-crowned Sparrows and Yellow-rumped Warblers are winter visitors. Red-shouldered and Cooper's Hawks nest in the area.

The northern end of Lower Crystal Springs Reservoir can be good for ducks (including an occasional Wood Duck) if enough marshy edge is exposed. Green Herons are uncommon migrants. Check any swallows carefully since all North American species with the exception of Cave Swallow are possible. Purple Martins are of rare but regular occurrence. A pair of them were recently found to be nesting at Pilarcitos Lake inside the watershed boundary. Check the Monterey Pines for Pygmy Nuthatches (resident) and Red-breasted Nuthatches (winter).

Open areas (grassy, oak and scrub) anywhere east of the reservoirs should be checked for raptors. Both species of eagles are rare but regular, White-tailed Kites are an uncommon resident and Peregrine Falcons and Merlins are rare from fall through spring. More common residents are California Thrashers, Western Meadowlarks, Pine Siskins, American and Lesser Goldfinches. In winter, look for Townsend's and Yellow-rumped Warblers, Fox Sparrows, Varied and Hermit Thrushes.

About half way down Sawyer Camp Trail, just north of Lower Crystal Springs Reservoir, is the famous Jepson Laurel. This 600 year old laurel is the oldest and largest laurel (California Bay) in California. It was named in honor of Willis Linn Jepson, one of California's most noted botanists.

Sawyer Camp Trail ends at Crystal Springs Road where you either have to retrace your steps or have a car waiting. You can then head south on Skyline and almost immediately cross Crystal Springs Dam. The dam and pullouts further south on Skyline should be used to scope Lower Crystal Springs Reservoir. In about 1 1/2 miles, at a stoplight, turn left and then, very shortly, take your first right onto Canada Road.

Use the pullouts on Cañada Road to scope Upper Crystal Springs Reservoir and observe woodland and open grassland species. In winter the open deep water of both these reservoirs can be good for Common Loons, Horned Grebes, Double-crested Cormorants, Common Goldeneyes, and Buffleheads. Less common, but occurring every year from fall through spring, are Common and Hooded Mergansers. At all seasons gulls bathe on the reservoirs in high numbers, and in winter you frequently can sight Herring, Thayer's, Mew and Bonaparte's Gulls. Check the shoreline for Great Blue Herons, Great Egrets, Spotted Sandpipers (all year), American Pipits, Common Snipe, Greater Yellowlegs and Belted Kingfishers (fall through spring). Canada Geese occur year round with a few pair nesting. Osprey are seen regularly during migration and occasionally in winter. Check all snags for Bald Eagles since one is present in most winters. There is varied habitat in the area and in the springtime this is a good place to find a variety of species such as Black Phoebe, Warbling Vireo, Purple Finch and Swainson's Thrush—which is more often heard than seen in the surrounding thickets.

Depending on water levels, dabbling ducks may be present in good numbers at the marshy south tip of the Upper Reservoir from fall through early winter. Look for Gadwalls, Green-winged Teal, Cinnamon Teal, Wood Ducks, Northern Pintails, Northern Shovelers, American Wigeons, Canvasbacks, Ring-necked Ducks, both Scaup species and Ruddy Ducks. Rare, but to be looked for, are: Eurasian Wigeons, Redheads, Barrow's Goldeneyes, Tundra Swans, Snow Geese and White-fronted Geese.

Continuing south on Cañada Road from the southern tip of the Upper Reservoir (the Pulgas Water Temple area) to Edgewood Road can be very productive but parking is limited. Residents in this area include Western Bluebirds (uncommon), White-breasted Nuthatches, Western Screech-Owls, Barn Owls, Acorn and Nuttall's Woodpeckers; A few Say's Phoebes can be found here in most winters. Wild Turkeys were introduced by the California Department of Fish and Game in the 1980's and a few are seen occasionally in the oaks.

A good way to see the area is by bicycle on the first or third Sunday of the month from April through October. On those days the road is closed to autos from Edgewood Road to Highway 92. Good destinations for the bike trip is the Pulgas Water Temple or the adjacent Filoli Estate.

The Filoli Estate is the property of the National Trust for Historic Preservation. Check by phone to determine when to visit or become involved with Friends of Filoli who carry out a variety of historic, horticultural, and nature education programs. The grounds of Filoli have a fine planted garden surrounded by large oaks and trails leading to riparian, redwood, and farm habitats. The area is surveyed regularly with 96 bird species considered part of Filoli's fauna and another 30 seen once or twice. Western Bluebirds usually breed in a nest box near the north entrance to Filoli. They are visible from Cañada Road. If you experience a sense of deja vu when you first see Filoli, don't be surprised. The building and grounds were featured in the opening credits of the television series, Dynasty.

Directions

When traveling **south** on I-280 take the Sneath Lane-San Bruno Avenue Exit. Go straight to San Bruno Avenue and turn right (west). When it dead ends turn left (south) on Skyline Boulevard (Highway 35). In about .6 mile you will see some pullouts and a parking area on the west side of the highway. This marks the north entrance to San Andreas Trail.

To reach the north entrance to the Sawyer Camp Trail continue south on Skyline until it merges with I-280 South. From here on for the next several miles, Skyline Boulevard either shares I-280 or parallels it and may be called Skyline Boulevard, Skyline Drive or Skyline Highway, depending on local usage. Take the first exit (Hillcrest, also marked Larkspur & Millbrae). Pass back under the freeway and turn right (south) on the frontage road (Skyline). Follow it to Hillcrest, turn right and park at the end. To reach the South end of the Sawyer Camp Trail, return to I-280 South and take the Black Mountain Road/Hayne Road exit. Turn right (west) and then, in a very short distance, left (south, on Skyline again). In about 1.3 miles you come to the Crystal Springs Road intersection and the south entrance to the Sawyer Camp Trail. Continuing south on Skyline, you come almost immediately to the Crystal Springs Dam, which also has parking. Continue south on Skyline, using the pullouts to scope Lower Crystal Springs Reservoir. At the stoplight (a little over a mile past the dam), you turn left (east) and follow the signs that lead you onto Cañada Road. Continue on Cañada Road which parallels the east side of Upper Crystal Springs Reservoir, again using the pullouts to scope the reservoir.

When traveling **north** on I-280, take the Highway 92/Half Moon Bay exit, at the stoplight turn right (north) on Skyline Hwy. 35. In about 1.3 mile you reach the Crystal Springs Road intersection and the south entrance to the Sawyer Camp Trail. Return to I-280 North either at Crystal Springs Road or at Black Mountain/Hayne Road (about 1.3 miles further on Skyline).

To reach the north entrance of the Sawyer Camp Trail, continue north on I-280 and take the Millbrae (Larkspur, Hillcrest) exit. Go straight (Skyline) and take the first left under the freeway (Hillcrest). The trail entrance is at its end. To reach the south entrance of the San Andreas Lake Trail, continue straight (north) on Skyline and turn left (west) on Larkspur. Re-enter I-280 North at Skyline and Larkspur. In less than a mile take the Pacifica-Skyline-Route 35 exit. In about .7 mile you'll find pullouts on either side of the road. San Andreas Reservoir and the north entrance to the San Andreas Trail are on your left.

Facilities

There are no restrooms on the San Andreas Lake Trail but several on the Sawyer Camp Trail. Gas stations are located nearby at the crests of Hillcrest Boulevard and Millbrae Avenue.

Dan Keller

California Sister Butterfly

SKYLINE BOULEVARD

❖

Dan Keller

Spring ★★★
Summer ★★★★
Fall ★★★
Winter ★★★

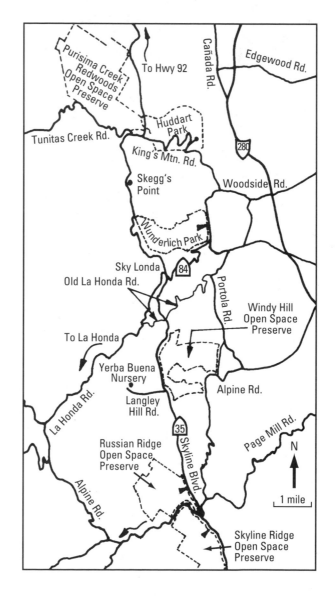

The portion of Skyline Boulevard (Highway 35) that begins at the summit of Highway 92 (connecting San Mateo and Half Moon Bay) and winds 19 miles south to the Santa Clara Line probably offers more variety in birding and nature watching than any other area in the county. Elevations between 500 and 2200 feet are easily accessible by driving one mile east or west. Habitats match this diversity in elevation and provide unexcelled birding. A drive down winding Skyline Boulevard can be enjoyed year-round, but perhaps the best time is spring and summer, when wildflowers and birds are in their glory. All the resident land birds can be found easily year-round with some very special species occurring nowhere else in San Mateo County.

This is the "main street" of the Midpeninsula Regional Open Space District, (MROSD) an independent governmental unit operating in San Mateo and Santa Clara Counties. Most of MROSD's preserves are located on or just off Skyline. POST, the Peninsula Open Space Trust, is a private non-profit organization that works closely with MROSD (and others) much as The Nature Conservancy works with state and federal agencies. Many of these parks are the result of the joint efforts of MROSD and POST.

MROSD identifies its preserves as belonging to Groups A and B. Group A preserves have parking areas, developed trails, signs and detailed trail maps. Group B preserves have little or no on-site parking, trails or roads that were in use at the time of acquisition and little or no signage. The letter in parentheses, i.e. "(A)" following the name identifies it as a District preserve and its status.

The **Purisima Creek Redwoods** Open Space Preserve (A) is located 4.5 miles south of the junction of State Highways 35 and 92 just beyond the Kings Mountain Country Store. This magnificent preserve harbors large redwoods, mixed conifers and wildflowers along almost 13 miles of trails. The habitat varies from fog-shrouded redwoods to rolling grasslands downslope. From here and anywhere to the south on Skyline you are likely to find breeding Hermit Warblers. Other uncommon nesters are Red-breasted Nuthatches and Hermit Thrushes. In winter this area is a great place for hawk watching. It's one of the better places to look for Golden Eagles. Band-tailed Pigeons, Common Ravens, Chestnut-backed Chickadees, Pine Siskins, Northern Pygmy-Owls and Steller's Jays are year- round residents. A second entrance 2.2 miles further south will put you more immediately into a forest of modestly-sized redwoods and Pacific Madrones.

Another 2.2 miles further south brings you to the **Skeggs Vista Point** on the east side of the highway. Park there and walk 150 yards north to the El Corte Madera Creek Open Space Preserve (B) on the west side of Skyline. This preserve is not identified by a sign, just a trailhead. This is a steep and heavily forested area, with some evidence of recent logging and some interesting sandstone formations. The birds are similar to those found at Purisima Creek.

Dan Keller

Pygmy Nuthatch

Determined hikers will find the "back door" to Wunderlich Park 1.4 miles south of Skegg's Vista Point. (See page 98 for the description of this park)

Old La Honda Road intersects Skyline 5.5 miles south of Skegg's Vista Point. Drive west .9 mile on this very narrow and winding road through a mixed forest area (where Winter Wrens, Hermit Thrushes and Northern Pygmy-Owls nest) to a steep dry rocky outcropping studded with monkeyflower, sage, Coyote Brush and Poison Oak. This highly specialized habitat is home for one of the county's most elusive nesting species: the Rufous-crowned Sparrow. First sighted in 1981, breeding was confirmed in 1992. Each year between 1 and 3 pairs nest in the steep slopes on either side of the road. Butterflies and wildflowers are abundant in Spring. Other interesting birds in this dry, unique habitat are Anna's and Allen's Hummingbirds, Ash-throated Flycatchers, California Thrashers, Nuttall's Woodpeckers, Western Meadowlarks and Lazuli Buntings. Less common but likely nesters are Lark Sparrows (in oaks near grasslands), Grasshopper Sparrows (grassland), and Black-throated Gray Warblers (oaks). Be very careful birding along this road. Very few automobiles use it, but it is a favorite for motorcyclists and bicyclists. Stop only at the pullouts and stay off the roadway when birding. After birding, find a safe place to turn around (try the wider private driveways about a mile further west) and return to Skyline.

The **Windy Hill Preserve** (A) parking lot is .9 miles south of Old La Honda Road on the east side of Skyline Boulevard. It is characterized by open grassland, large rolling hills, wildflowers and native grasses. The open views are great for hawk watching year-round. Walk the trail to the left from the parking lot (Spring Ridge Trail). In about ½ mile you will come to a cypress grove, once the site of a farmhouse. One or two pairs of House Wrens can usually be found in the summer. Look for them in the dead snags. This is one of only a few nesting places in San Mateo County. This is probably the easiest place in the county to find Lazuli Buntings (up to 5 pairs nest annually). Other birds are Lesser and American Goldfinches, Pine Siskins, Song and Savannah Sparrows and Bewick's Wrens. This is a fine place to study native plants. In winter this is another good place to look for those erratic wanderers—Red Crossbills and Evening Grosbeaks.

Langley Hill Road is west of Skyline 2.3 miles south of Windy Hill, opposite the Tom Fogerty Winery. At .6 miles stop at the big pullout on your left and bird up and down the road, at least 100 yards. This is a good place for Hermit Warblers (migrant) Black-throated Gray Warblers, Olive-sided Flycatchers, Western Wood-Pewees, Solitary Vireos, Hutton's Vireos, Hairy Woodpeckers, and less commonly, Chipping Sparrows (all summer) and Golden-crowned Kinglets (year-round). At night both Northern Pygmy-Owls and Western Screech-Owls can be heard here. Continue down the road to the **Yerba Buena Nursery**. The Nursery (open 9–5 daily) is a wonderful place. Devoted to California native plants only, it offers a plant display garden and some outstanding birding. If you have only two hours to bird in spring this is the place to go. Birders are generously allowed to bird all over the nursery. Be sure to check the ponds, one above the parking lot and the other down behind the old barn. Birds to be expected are Black Phoebes, Ash-throated Flycatchers, Pacific-Slope Flycatchers, Western Wood-Pewees, Acorn, Downy, Hairy and Nuttall's Woodpeckers, Northern Flickers, Red-tailed Hawks, Cooper's Hawks (a pair nests nearby), Orange-crowned, Wilson's and Yellow Warblers, Hutton's and Warbling Vireos, Allen's and Anna's Hummingbirds, Song Sparrows,

Swainson's Thrushes, Dark-eyed Junco, Black-headed Grosbeaks, Pine Siskins and American Goldfinches. In winter be sure to look for Winter Wrens, Ruby-crowned and Golden-crowned Kinglets, Hermit and Varied Thrushes, Golden-crowned and White-crowned Sparrows, Fox Sparrows and perhaps Red Crossbills. Most winters you can find Red-breasted Sapsuckers in the orchard across from the barn.

Continue on south 1.8 miles to the Russian Ridge and Skyline Ridge Open Space Preserves (A) at the intersection with Alpine Road.

Facilities

There are restrooms at the parking lots of the "(A)" preserves and at the Yerba Buena Nursery. See the end of the next article for more information.

Mary Molteni

Purple Finch

RUSSIAN RIDGE AND SKYLINE RIDGE OPEN SPACE PRESERVES

❖

Anne Scanlan-Rohrer, Frank and Jean Allen
Updated by Dan Keller and Cliff Richer

Spring ★★★

Summer ★★★★

Fall ★★★

Winter ★★★

The Russian Ridge Open Space Preserve (A) consists of 1455 acres lying south and west of the intersection of Alpine Road and Skyline Drive. The parking lot entrance is on Alpine Road less than a hundred yards off of Skyline.

The preserve is primarily grassland habitat. Some say that the best wildflower display on Skyline Drive is found on this preserve. Six miles of trails (1993), with more planned, begin at the parking lot The Ridge Trail which parallels Skyline Boulevard affords the best views and spring wildflowers, while the Mindego Ridge Trail, which branches off of the Ridge Trail drops 700 feet in less than 2 miles to take you into oak woodland forest.

This preserve is particularly attractive to mountain bicyclists and you should keep this in mind as most of the trails are quite narrow.

The Skyline Ridge Open Space Preserve (A) can also be accessed from this same parking lot. A pedestrian walkway takes you under Alpine Road to Alpine Pond and to the best birding areas of the preserve. When you enter the preserve at the Alpine Road entrance, you are likely to be greeted by calls of California Quail, Acorn Woodpeckers, Northern Flickers, White-breasted Nuthatches, Steller's and Scrub Jays. Walk on the dirt path around Alpine Lake to see Violet-green and Barn Swallows (summer) dashing over the lake. The Daniels Nature Center on the shore of Alpine Pond is the most concrete example of the interaction of the Midpeninsula Open Space District and the Peninsula Open Space Trust. Brochures at the entrance explain the workings of this cooperative venture more fully.

You can take the Ridge Trail south and east to the grassland and scrub areas. This trail generally follows the 2200' contour line about 1½ miles to the parking lot at the main entrance. You can also take the Page Mill Trail which drops about 500' in 1½ miles into oak forest for Downy Woodpeckers, Hutton's Vireos, and Bewick's Wrens. Flocks of Band-tailed Pigeons fly overhead frequently. But the best birding is along a series of short unnamed trails that take you to the ranger facility at the site of the original farm buildings. The varied habitat to and about ½ mile beyond the ranger facility will generally provide most of the species that can be seen on the preserve.

The main entrance to this 1250 acre preserve is located .9 miles south of the Alpine-Skyline intersection on Skyline on the site of what was only recently a Christmas tree farm. There are three large parking lots here; one designed to accommodate handicapped parking; one for equestrians and their horse trailers; and one for the general public. Horseshoe Lake is easily accessible by wheelchair from the handicapped parking area and by foot or horseback from either of the other lots. You can also access the Ridge Trail from the general parking lot and follow it and other paths to the ranger facility and to Alpine Pond.

Visitors to the preserve can look down from one of its many high points to view a wilderness area comprised of chaparral, coastal scrub, grasslands, small lakes, and mixed evergreen forest. The forest is dominated by Canyon Live Oak, and also includes California Bay, Bigleaf Maple, Pacific Madrone, and Tan Oak.

The variety of habitats appear to attract an equally diverse bird population. Summer birding is excellent and many of the birds here are more typical of the Sierras. Red-breasted Nuthatches, Western Tanagers, Lazuli Buntings, Lark and Chipping Sparrows, Red Crossbills, and Yellow-rumped Warblers with young have all been seen here in the summer. There is also a record of a Calliope Hummingbird, one of a handful for the county.

Birds to Look For

Year-round Residents
Turkey Vulture, Red-shouldered Hawk, Red-tailed Hawk, Cooper's Hawk, California Quail, Band-tailed Pigeon, Mourning Dove, Great Horned Owl, Northern Pygmy-Owl, Western Screech-Owl, Anna's Hummingbird, Northern Flicker, Downy, Hairy, Nuttall's and Acorn Woodpeckers, Steller's and Scrub Jay, Common Raven, Winter Wren, Chestnut-backed Chickadee, Plain Titmouse, Bushtit, White-breasted and Pygmy Nuthatches, Brown Creeper, Wrentit, Bewick's Wren, California Thrasher, Hutton's Vireo, House and Purple Finches, Rufous-sided and California Towhees, Song Sparrow, Dark-eyed Junco, American and Lesser Goldfinches, and Pine Siskin.

Summer Breeders
Allen's Hummingbird, (Rufous Hummingbird is a common migrant), Warbling Vireo, (Cassin's) Solitary Vireo, Pacific-slope Flycatcher, Ash-throated and Olive-sided Flycatchers, Western Wood-Pewee, Black-throated Gray, Orange-crowned, Wilson's and in the highest areas Hermit Warblers (uncommon), Black-headed Grosbeak, American Robin, and Swainson's Thrush.

Winter Visitors
Ruby-crowned and Golden-crowned Kinglets, Red-breasted Sapsucker, Sharp-shinned Hawk, Northern Saw-whet Owl, Varied Thrush, Hermit Thrush, Fox Sparrow, Golden-crowned and White-crowned Sparrows. In some years you'll find Red Crossbills in the higher elevations.

Directions

If you are coming from the north follow the directions from the previous article. If you are coming from the south you may wish to take a more direct route. From Highway 101 or Interstate 280 take Highway 84 (Woodside Road) west through the town of Woodside to the intersection of Highway 84 with Skyline Boulevard (Highway 35). Take Skyline south approximately seven miles to its intersection with Page Mill and Alpine Roads. Turn right (west) onto Alpine Road for the Russian Ridge entrance or continue .9 miles beyond the intersection for the main Skyline Ridge entrance.

Facilities

There are restrooms at all parking lots. Service stations and restaurants can be found at the intersection of Skyline Boulevard and Highway 84, and in the town of Woodside.

Nearby points of interest

Following Alpine Road further west will take you to Portola State Park, Sam McDonald County Park, Pescadero Creek County Park, and San Mateo County Memorial Park. Heading east, Highway 84 passes through Woodside and leads past the entrance roads to both Huddart County Park and Wunderlich Park. Huddart, Wunderlich, Portola and Pescadero Creek Parks are described in the next three chapters. Sam McDonald and Memorial Parks, like Pescadero Creek and Portola, are densely wooded redwood forest and offer the same kinds of habitat.

HUDDART COUNTY PARK

❖

Donna Kirsacko
Updated By Dan Keller

Spring ★★★
Summer ★★★
Fall ★★★
Winter ★★★

Huddart County Park is one of San Mateo County's most versatile recreation areas. The 973 acres offer the opportunity to bird in redwood/Douglas Fir forest, oak woodland, Pacific Madrone and California Bay associations, as well as creek side and riparian habitats. Bird life is plentiful and diverse.

Common year-round residents include Red-tailed Hawk, California Quail, Hairy and Downy Woodpeckers, Nuttall's Woodpecker, White-breasted, Red-breasted and Pygmy Nuthatches, Brown Creeper, Bewick's Wren, California Thrasher, and the usual complement of hummingbirds, titmice, chickadees, juncos and Wrentits. Mid-elevation birds in summer are Pacific-Slope Flycatcher, Olive-sided Flycatcher, Western Wood-Pewee, Swainson's Thrush, Cassin's race of the Solitary Vireo, Black-throated Gray, Wilson's and Orange-crowned Warblers. In winter one can also find Ruby-crowned Kinglet, Red-breasted Sapsucker, Varied and Hermit Thrushes, Fox Sparrow, Golden-crowned, White-crowned and Lincoln's Sparrows. At night listen for Northern Saw-whet Owl in mixed conifer forests, and Western Screech-Owl in lower elevation oaks.

The park is open year-round from dawn to dusk. Birding in the fall and winter when park use is light can be rewarding. Huddart Park has an extensive hiking trail system, group and individual picnic areas, equestrian trails, and even an archery range. There is a trailhead off Kings Mountain Road west of the main entrance, and another trailhead north of the intersection of Kings Mountain Road and Skyline Boulevard on Skyline. Be sure to park without blocking driveways, and watch for "no parking anytime" signs. There is also a trail through the California Water Company–Bear Gulch Watershed paralleling Skyline Boulevard, which connects Huddart Park with Wunderlich Park.

Directions

Huddart County Park's main entrance is off Kings Mountain Road in Woodside. From Interstate 280 exit at Woodside Road West (Highway 84) and proceed west for approximately 1.5 miles. Veer right onto Kings Mountain Road and follow it for two miles (the road winds considerably) to the main entrance on your right.

Facilities

There are restroom facilities and running water; consult maps available at the park entrance for exact locations of facilities and trails. Food is available in Woodside. The park has many attractive and inviting picnic groves with tables and barbecue facilities.

Fee

There is a an entrance fee per vehicle. Collection of this fee is somewhat erratic, but currently the rule of thumb is to count on the fee being collected only on weekends and holidays. Reservations are needed in advance for the group picnic grounds.

Dan Keller

Nuttall's Woodpecker

WUNDERLICH PARK

❖

Jean and Frank Allen
Revised By Dan Keller

Spring ★★★

Summer ★

Fall ★★★

Winter ★★★

Wunderlich Park was created in 1974 through a gift of 942 acres of coniferous forest and meadows. Between 1850 and 1870 the large redwoods in this area were cut to build San Francisco. The lumber was hauled to the bay in Redwood City, and sailed by schooner to San Francisco. The lowlands around Wunderlich Park were farmed, and the hillside forests were allowed to acquire a second growth. James A. Folger, the second owner of the farmlands, built the handsome stable across from the parking lot in early 1900. Martin Wunderlich, the third owner, acquired much of the Folger estate in 1956 and in 1974 generously gave 942 acres to San Mateo County for open space and park use. Today, the county has completed 25 miles of trails, and it is possible to walk 10 miles from Skyline Boulevard down to the park or select any of several shorter loops.

The park is open year-round from 8:00 A.M. until dusk, and there is usually a park ranger on duty. Birding is best in spring. Wunderlich is heavily oriented toward equestrian use, so when you're birding here, you are expected to step aside for riders and to avoid startling the horses. The many trails are described in detail in *Peninsula Trails* by Jean Rusmore and Frances Spangle.

Connecting trails make it possible to walk loops from one to ten miles long through mixed woodlands of Black Oaks, Toyons, Canyon Oaks and Pacific Madrones, which may yield the same general bird species as described under Huddart Park, above.

In the spring, Douglas Iris, poppies, Sword Fern, Goldback Fern, and Giant Chain Fern (woodwardia) decorate the trails. Baby Blue-eyes, lupines, Hound's Tongue, Milk Maids, Indian Warrior, Sticky Monkeyflower, Hazelnut, California Buckeye, and gooseberry also thrive in the shady forest. Other native plants may be seen in the well-kept Native Plant Garden behind the Woodside Library on Woodside Road near town.

Directions

Take Interstate 280 to the Highway 84 (Woodside Road) exit and turn west. From the town of Woodside after Woodside Road, Highway 84 turns south; look for Bear Gulch Road. About one-quarter mile past it you will see the small park sign on the right. This is 1.7 miles from the Woodside Town Hall.

Facilities

There are portable toilets at the parking lot for Wunderlich Park. Gas stations and restaurants can be found in the nearby towns of Woodside and Portola Valley.

Dan Keller

Black-throated Gray Warbler

PORTOLA STATE PARK AND PESCADERO CREEK COUNTY PARKS

❖

Al DeMartini

Spring ★★★
Summer ★★
Fall ★★
Winter ★★★

Portola State Park and the Pescadero Creek County Park complex (made up of four contiguous parks, Pescadero Creek, Memorial, Sam McDonald and the Heritage Grove) are located on the upper Pescadero and Alpine Creek watersheds.

These under-birded parks offer ample opportunities for the study of natural history as well as fine scenery and trails and are easily reached from either Skyline Boulevard (Highway 35) or the coastal route (Highway 1). From the coast both La Honda Road (Highway 84) and Pescadero Road provide access while from Skyline either La Honda Road (heading roughly SW) or Alpine Road can be taken. These routes are all winding and scenic, but Alpine Road offers finer panoramas of the varied landscapes and vegetation and has dazzling ocean views. By using pullouts on Alpine and the Portola cutoff Road

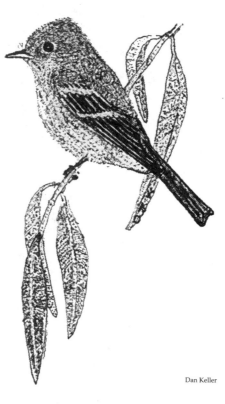

Dan Keller

Pacific-slope Flycatcher

one can scan for raptors etc. and appreciate the wide range of habitats in the area—valleys and wetter slopes cloaked in a grand forest of Coastal Redwood; Douglas Fir with drier slopes; hills covered by grassland, chaparral or a forest of Douglas Fir, live oak and Pacific Madrone. Among Bay Area birders, Portola especially is known as the most likely spot in the County to see such locally scarce residents as Pileated Woodpecker (along Coyote Ridge Trail or near ranger's residence #1 near the Portola Park boundary) American Dipper (along Pescadero and Peter's Creek) and Vaux's Swift (a pair nests in the chimney of the Visitor Center some years!). The endangered Marbled Murrelet is also present, mainly as a breeding bird. It is possible to catch a glimpse of these treetop nesting seabirds and hear them call as they fly overhead from April to August. A good place to listen in and perhaps see them as they return to the nest is in the clearing around residence #1 at or just before daybreak.

Year-round residents include Band-tailed Pigeon, Belted Kingfisher, Acorn & Hairy Woodpeckers, Northern Flicker, both jays, Common Raven, Chestnut-backed Chickadee, Plain Titmouse, Bushtit, Red-breasted and Pygmy Nuthatches, Brown Creeper, Bewick's and Winter Wrens, Golden-crowned Kinglet, Hermit Thrush, Wrentit, California Thrasher (the last two in chaparral), Hutton's Vireo, Hermit Warbler (very rare in most winters), both Towhees, Dark-eyed Junco, Purple Finch, Pine Siskin and Lesser Goldfinch. Varied Thrush, previously thought to be only a winter visitor, was recently discovered as a rare and secretive breeder in this area and so should probably be considered year-round residents, even though it is far more common in winter. Listen for its song at dawn in the conifers.

Breeding birds, present from March through August include Vaux's Swift, Allen's Hummingbird, Western Wood-Pewee, Pacific-slope Flycatcher, Swainson's Thrush (in riparian areas), Warbling Vireo, Orange-crowned, Black-throated Gray, and Wilson's Warblers.

Among the winter birds are Red-breasted Sapsucker, Ruby-crowned Kinglet, Townsend's Warbler, and Fox Sparrow. Raptors are more common in winter and in fall migration so keep a lookout for Sharp-shinned and Cooper's Hawks, soaring Red-tailed Hawk, American Kestrel hunting the open roadside areas and even Golden Eagle. Also notable are the variety of owls to be heard and, if lucky, seen. Western Screech, Great Horned Owl, Northern Pygmy-Owl and Saw-whet Owl are all present in the area with the very rare possibility of a Spotted Owl (based on one recent report, as well as scattered reports through the years of these owls having been seen and heard throughout the area). Then, too, there is always the rare chance of encountering montane vagrants such as Townsend's Solitaire and Clark's Nutcracker. Cattle Egrets have been seen following livestock on ranches just outside of Portola as well.

While it is possible to bird some of the area by car, the extensive trail network of these interlinked parks beckons the walking birder. The Coyote Ridge and Iverson trails of Portola and the Pomponio trail linking the county and state parks especially recommend themselves to birders but others of the twenty-plus trails should be explored as well. A day is probably enough to cover many good areas in either park. Historically, Portola has been less disturbed by extraction and has more old-growth than Pescadero and should be more productive but Pescadero has been less thoroughly explored by birders and so may yield some surprises. For those with more time a variety of camping options are available. Car camping sites at Portola can be reserved (415-948-9098) while Memorial Park's sites are first-come first-served (call 415-879-0212 for camp information). Reservations are required for the Jack Brook Horse camp and two back country trail camps (Shaw Flat and Tarwater) Call Pescadero Park (415-363-4021) as well as the Slate Creek Trail Camp in Portola (415-948-9098). Maps and current trail information are available at both Portola and Memorial Park ranger stations.

Dan Keller

Common Yellowthroat

THE COASTSIDE

❖

California Highway One, also called the Coast Highway, runs along the entire length of the San Mateo coast. The best birding spots are either on or very close to Highway One. The Santa Cruz Mountains and the reservoirs of San Andreas Valley isolate the coast from the more populous Bayshore. As a consequence, the difficulty of crossing to the coast has kept the area south of Half Moon Bay relatively undeveloped. Several narrow and winding roads (Highway 84, for example) cross to the ocean, but the main cross-peninsula road is Highway 92 from San Mateo to Half Moon Bay.

Highway One is the principal access from either the north or south. If you're coming south from San Francisco take 19th Avenue or the Central Freeway (I-80) to Interstate 280. Follow I-280 south to the Pacifica Exit. Take the Pacifica Exit. You are now on Highway One.

The Coast Highway is also accessible by driving on Skyline Drive from Lake Merced or Fort Funston in San Francisco. Just follow Skyline Drive south to the Highway One exit.

If you're anxious to get in some birding or check for oceanic species, take the second Pacifica exit and follow city streets to the Pacific Ocean and the Pacifica Municipal Fishing Pier. There is ample parking south of the pier at Sharp Park Beach.

All three scoters and all three commonly occurring loons can be seen in winter near the Fishing Pier. Alcids and shearwaters have also been seen feeding here in late summer and fall. A freshwater marsh on the Sharp Park golf course is accessible by walking the levee south from Sharp Park Beach. This marsh is home to the usual marsh species and contributes considerable diversity to Pacifica's bird population. After checking these areas return to Highway One.

SWEENEY RIDGE

❖

The Western Access—Pacifica
Wanda Belland Updated by Carol Miller

Spring ★★★

Summer ★

Fall ★★★

Winter ★★★

Sweeney Ridge lies at the northern end of the San Francisco watershed area between San Bruno and Pacifica. These 1047 acres comprise one eighth of the land mass of the city of Pacifica. Sweeney Ridge became part of the Golden Gate National Recreation Area in February 1984.

There are a number of trails leading through the area; however, the Fassler Avenue entrance trail appears to be the trail of choice for many, especially history buffs who wish to follow in the footsteps of Portola. This trail originates in Pacifica.

From Highway One take Fassler Avenue east to its end at a cyclone fence. Park on the street and enter the area through the footpath through the fence. The first three-quarters mile of the trail rises steeply and can be considered a moderate to strenuous climb, depending on your physical condition. Immediately after the trail head, you will see a water tank on your left. It is surrounded by evergreens and may have flocks of birds, especially during spring and fall migrations. Continue past the water tank, staying to the right at the fork in the road. Stop every now and then to check the skies for Red-tailed Hawks, Turkey Vultures, Sharp-shinned Hawks, Cooper's Hawks, and American Kestrels. Keep your eyes to the skies, as other hawks may be seen along this coastal corridor, particularly in the fall.

Upon reaching the top, approximately ¾–1 mile, stop to rest and enjoy the beautiful views of the Pacific coast. Check on top of, in, and around the Coyote Brush for White-crowned Sparrows, Fox Sparrows, Wrentits, Song Sparrows, California and Rufous-sided Towhees and Savannah Sparrows. At this point the toughest part of the trail is behind you. Wildflowers abound in April. Splashes of bright orange California Poppies, Checker-bloom, Blue-eyed Grass, Blue Dicks, mules ears, Footsteps of Spring, sun cups, buttercups, columbine, indian paintbrushes, Cream Cups and goldfields dot the terrain. Many grasses also cover the coastal hills, along with Coyote Brush, Cow Parsnip, *Ceanothus*, Poison Oak, Wax Myrtle, soap plant, California Figwort, and various thistles.

From the top of the hill, continue in an eastward direction through a red metal fence. Listen for the familiar "bouncing ball" song of the Wrentits. Look for Mourning Doves, Brewer's Blackbirds, Brown-headed Cowbirds and an occasional Loggerhead Shrike. Western Meadowlarks dot the grasses and California Quail, hummingbirds, American Robins, Common Ravens, American Crows and several species of swallows can be found here.

Stay to the left at the power lines, always proceeding on the main trail. Stop at the rock outcropping along the road to admire and examine the myriad small wildflowers, ferns, mosses, lichens, and succulents.

Continuing on, you will come to a two-way split in the road. Take the left fork, always staying on the main large trail. This will lead to the Portola Discovery Site and Skyline Ridge. When you reach the site, spend some time there. You will know the site by the monuments erected there to Gaspar de Portola's Expedition of 1769 and the Carl McCarthy Memorial Monument. Portola and his men made the first trip up Sweeney Ridge where they discovered San Francisco Bay 215 years ago. Carl McCarthy was one of those instrumental in founding the Portola Foundation and the driving force in the establishment of the Portola Discovery Site as a historical landmark. Enjoy the spectacular view. The Discovery Site is approximately one and a half miles from Fassler Avenue.

This trail you have just climbed is called the Baquiano trail, but unfortunately there are no signs until you are near the Portola Discovery Site. Trails and roads are not marked very clearly and when fog shrouds these coastal hills, it is very easy to lose one's bearings. Many trails and roads crisscross. A compass is advisable. Climbing on summer afternoons can be chancy as the fog can roll in very quickly and can be absolutely impenetrable. Strong winds are also typical of summer afternoons in the area and the combination can make the return very hazardous. More than one climber has had to be rescued by Pacifica's fire department. It is not a coincidence that Pacifica provides mountain and coastal rescue specialists for the entire county.

During the spring, there are huge areas of wild iris in bloom, with colors ranging from white through deep purple. There is a road south of the Discovery Site along the ridge. Watch for Scrub Jays and Northern Mockingbirds along this road. Gulls and ducks fly overhead to and from the Spring Valley Lakes and inland waters. This road, the Sweeney Ridge Trail, follows the ridge approximately three quarters of a mile south to where one encounters the locked Portola Ridge Gate. The property beyond is owned by the San Francisco Water District and special permission must be obtained for extensive access to these lands. There is limited access near the gate.

Backtracking to the Portola Discovery Site, look for deer and rabbits at sunset. This site is also the end point for the trail which originates on the eastern flank of Sweeney Ridge. From the Discovery Site, retrace your steps to the barbed wire barricade. From this point it is easy to take the wrong road; stay to the left at the fork. The entire hike is approximately five miles, and takes about four hours to walk, with stops for snacks, birds, and wildflowers. The Ridge may also be reached from the East. See the Sweeney Ridge—Eastern Access section of this book for more details.

Directions

Pacifica is ten miles south of San Francisco on Coastal Route One (follow the signs to Pacifica from Interstate 280 South); turn left (inland) at the second traffic signal onto Fassler Avenue. There is a Shell gas station on the left corner as you make the turn. Drive to the end of Fassler Avenue (Approximately $1\frac{1}{2}$ miles) and park your car on the residential streets in front of the cyclone fence barricade. There is a break in the fence which you can walk through. This is the start of the trail.

Facilities

There are no facilities on Sweeney Ridge itself. Gas stations and restaurants can be found close by in Pacifica.

Note: The map for this section may be found with the "Sweeney Ridge—The Eastern Access" section on page 79.

SAN PEDRO VALLEY COUNTY PARK

❖

Scott Smithson
Updated by Judy Spitler

Spring ★★★
Summer ★★
Fall ★★★
Winter ★★★

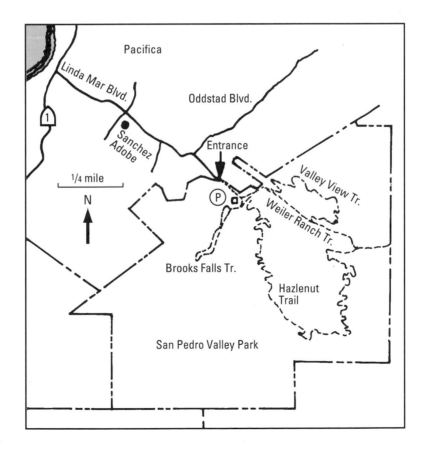

San Pedro Valley County Park is a beautiful wilderness area located in the foothills of the Santa Cruz Mountain Range in the city of Pacifica. The park's variety of plants and wildlife brings enjoyment to all levels of nature lovers.

The park's trails are very well-marked, and there are good maps available at the Visitors' Center. There are four well-traveled short trails in the park: the Old Trout Farm Trail, the Brooks Falls Overlook Trail, Weiler Ranch Road and the Valley View Trail. These trails abound with plants and wildlife.

There are three longer trails: the Hazelnut Trail, a circular trail that begins on the Plaskon Nature Trail behind the Visitor Center and ends on the Weiler Ranch Road, and the Montara Mountain Trail, a 6 mile trail that eventually takes you to Montara State Beach. Both have substantial elevation gains, and the Montara Mountain Trail has spectacular views. The other long trail, the Brooks Creek Trail, could be investigated, also. These longer trails are primarily for hikers and you'll mostly see the coastal scrub species: Wrentits, Song Sparrows, Scrub Jays, Bushtits and Rufous-sided and California Towhees. Occasionally you will get a great view of a soaring hawk and you have a better chance of seeing a California Thrasher along these trails. In the summer, Anna's and Allen's Hummingbirds abound. Nevertheless, the greatest diversity of bird life is found in the valley along the shorter trails.

The Old Trout Farm Trail yields a variety of birds, mainly because it parallels the willow bushes and riparian areas along Brooks Creek. This trail is broad and level and is .8 miles long. In the spring and summer, Swainson's Thrushes, Black-headed Grosbeaks, Hutton's Vireos, Warbling Vireos and Solitary Vireos can be seen. The largest concentration of warblers in the park is found on this trail. Orange-crowned and Wilson's Warblers are common summer residents. Hermit, Black-throated Gray, Nashville and Yellow Warblers are seen during the spring and fall migration seasons. In late fall and winter, notable species such as Winter Wrens, Varied Thrushes, Hermit Thrushes, Golden-crowned and Ruby-crowned Kinglets, Yellow-rumped and Townsend's Warblers, and Fox Sparrows inhabit the Old Trout Farm Trail. Year-round residents include Northern Flickers, Steller's Jays, Chestnut-sided Chickadees, Bushtits, California Towhees, Dark-eyed Juncos, Rufous-sided Towhee, Bewick's Wren and Song Sparrows. Always keep an eye out for Cooper's and Sharp-shinned Hawks in this area of the park.

The Brooks Falls Overlook Trail starts in the same kind of habitat as does the Old Trout Farm Trail. It then runs up the hillside into brushy areas with scattered young pine and eucalyptus trees. This .7 mile hike is significant because of the beautiful overlook of Brooks Falls, a seasonal waterfall. The falls flow into Brooks Creek, a feeder stream to the south fork of San Pedro Creek, which is tapped annually by the North Coast County Water District to provide

10% of Pacifica's drinking water. In spring and summer, Allen's, Anna's and sometimes Rufous Hummingbirds can be seen on this trail. Pacific-slope Flycatchers are especially common during this season of the year. Song Sparrows, Chestnut-backed Chickadees, Downy Woodpeckers, Wrentits and Bushtits are year-round residents.

The Plaskon Nature Trail is a very short trail beginning about a hundred feet to the right of the Visitor's Center as you face it. It crosses Brooks Creek and provides an entry into the creek's riparian area. This trail can be checked when you're traveling between the valley trails described above and those described below. Also be sure to check the area directly behind the Visitor Center. Bushtits and chickadees can almost always be found here and they are occasionally accompanied by feeding warblers and vireos.

The Weiler Ranch Road is the other wide, level trail in the park. This 1.4-mile trail goes through a rather dry area. There are beautiful meadows to the south and grass-covered hills to the north. At the beginning of the trail, check the Walnut Grove Group Picnic Area. In the spring and summer, this area provides excellent habitat for Olive-sided Flycatchers, Purple Finches, House Finches, Pine Siskins, American Goldfinches, and Lesser Goldfinches. In the winter Dark-eyed Juncos and Fox Sparrows are very fond of this grove. Hairy Woodpeckers, Downy Woodpeckers and Red-breasted Sapsuckers (winter only for Sapsucker) love the walnut trees. The rest of the Weiler Ranch Road is straight and level. Spring and summer birds expected on this part of the trail include Orange-crowned Warblers, Black-headed Grosbeaks, and Western Wood-Pewees. California Quail, Scrub Jays, Wrentits, Bewick's Wrens, California Towhees, and Song Sparrows are all year-round residents. California Thrashers are becoming more common on this trail, but are more frequently heard on the Montara Mountain Trail. Aerial birds such as Red-tailed Hawks, Turkey Vultures, and American Kestrels can be seen flying overhead. Golden Eagles have also been seen over the park, but they are a rarity.

The Valley View Trail is much like the Weiler Ranch Road, except that it is somewhat longer, more winding and has some incline. This 1.6 mile trail has the same species of birds as does the Weiler Ranch Road. Wildflowers are the special attractions here. Look for them in the spring. Unfortunately, the trail also is also noted for Poison Oak. Many mammals can be found on both the Valley View Trail and the Weiler Ranch Road. Mule Deer, Brush Rabbits, Bobcats, Gray Foxes, and Striped Skunks are a few that may be seen in this grassland area.

Great Horned Owls are common in the park and are often heard at dusk. Barn Owls are seen regularly but may be visitors from known nesting areas outside the park. Western Screech-Owls, Northern Saw-whet Owls and Northern Pygmy-Owls have been heard calling but their overall status is unknown as this is primarily a day-use facility. There is anecdotal evidence that

Screech-Owls nest in the park. In Spring of 1993 a hiker followed a deer trail, lost his way and had to spend the night entangled in a thicket. He reported waking at dawn to find two young Screech-Owls examining him with wide-eyed curiosity from a low-lying branch.

Directions

Take Coastal Route 1 to the city of Pacifica, 10 miles south of San Francisco. Turn east on Linda Mar Boulevard. At its end, turn right on Oddstad Boulevard, and make an immediate left into the Park.

Facilities

The park has three restroom facilities. Service stations and restaurants are located one block north on Oddstad Boulevard in Park Mall. There is a Visitors' Center with an excellent exhibition area and a public phone beside its entrance. The exhibits are arranged by the five major plant communities that are found in the park. By using stuffed animals and pressed plants, the displays point out the plants and wildlife of each community. Wheelchairs are available. The Trout Farm Trail and the Weiler Ranch Road are both wheelchair accessible for most of their length.

Fee

There is a vehicle entrance fee, currently collected only on weekends. There is no fee for walk-in visitors.

Publications

There are free trail maps and checklists for birds (recently updated), mammals, plants, and flowers available in the Visitors' Center. The center is normally open on the weekends and may be open on other days, depending on the availability of volunteer staffing. The center has a small, but surprisingly good, reference library with a comfortable reading area. You can purchase field guides, other books and environmentally-oriented articles at the counter and there are plans for a modest gift shop. The Visitors' Center also stocks brochures for other county parks. The phone number for the park headquarters is (415) 355-6489.

Nearby Points of Interest

The Sanchez Adobe, located west of the park on Linda Mar Boulevard is one of the oldest buildings in northern California. Lovingly restored, it is visited by thousands of school children and tourists each year. You can visit other birding areas in Pacifica if you have time. You can view water birds and shorebirds at San Pedro State Beach at the western end of Linda Mar just across Route 1. A Red-footed Booby became a major local attraction when it made a two week visit to San Pedro Rock off Pedro Point just south of an Pedro State Beach in August of 1987.

PRINCETON HARBOR AND PILLAR POINT

❖

Peter J. Metropulos

Spring ★★★★
Summer ★★★
Fall ★★★★
Winter ★★★★

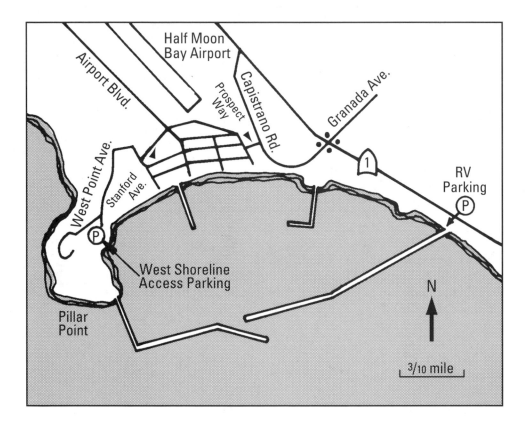

Princeton Harbor is the only protected harbor on the coast between San Francisco and Santa Cruz. A series of breakwaters running south and east of Pillar Point encloses the harbor, situated at the north end of Half Moon Bay.

A prime birding location, its abundance and diversity are greatest in winter and fall. It is worthy of a half to full day of your time. Since this is a bustling harbor, human activity can greatly affect birding success. Weekdays and periods of bad weather, when human traffic is low, are most productive.

The best area for birding is the protected northwest corner, reached as follows: from Coast Highway One, turn west at the stoplight at Capistrano Road and continue along the north side of the harbor to Prospect Way. Turn left onto Harvard Avenue and proceed through the boat yards to West Point Avenue which curves around a marshy area and heads uphill to an Air Force Radar Facility. You will find the "West Shoreline Access" parking lot below the radar station. Be sure to look over the marsh before continuing on. When it is in a wet condition it serves as a stop-over point for small numbers of migrant shorebirds and waterfowl. Uncommon but regular in August and September are Baird's and Pectoral Sandpipers and Lesser Yellowlegs. Red Phalaropes may be blown into the marsh during windy storms from October to December. Common Yellowthroats, Marsh Wrens, Virginia Rails, Soras and Lincoln's Sparrows are regular here. In the winter Tricolored Blackbirds often roost by the hundreds in the dense rushes and cattails. During the day they can be found feeding in freshly cultivated fields in the vicinity of the nearby airport. The willow thickets here are difficult to bird since there are no trails entering them and the area is full of Poison Oak and Stinging Nettles but birding along their edges can be productive. The dense vegetation here—rich in insects, weeds and cover— attracts migrant songbirds, and many vagrant species (most notably "eastern" warblers) have been observed, mainly in September and October.

Head south from the marsh and the parking lot and follow the dirt trail below the cliffs and toward the jetties. Scan the harbor for loons, grebes, cormorants, and sea ducks. Oldsquaws, Brants, and Red-necked Grebes are regular. The very rare Yellow-billed Loon has been observed here and should be looked for in the winter. During late summer and fall schools of fish often concentrate in the harbor and provide feeding grounds for large numbers of Brown Pelicans, Elegant Terns, and Heermann's Gulls. During this season one or two Parasitic Jaegers may be spotted near the jetties, keeping a watchful eye out for fish-carrying terns. Common Murres and Pigeon Guillemots often are present near the harbor entrance or in the bay beyond, and a few Marbled Murrelets are often found further out on the bay. Of irregular occurrence, small numbers of Ancient Murrelets have been seen here in some winters as well. Other species of alcids such as Rhinoceros Auklet and Tufted Puffin occur offshore, and should be looked for with a spotting scope when weather conditions and visibility are suitable. Also be on the lookout for a sea otter in the kelp beds.

Where the dirt trail reaches the first jetty you will see Pillar Point Reef to the west. Low tides will expose a flat rocky reef north of the jetty. This reef is rich and diverse in intertidal marine life, and consequently is quite popular with fishermen, beachcombers and marine biology students. Several Harbor Seals are usually loafing about on the higher rocks. The exposed reef may be teeming with foraging shorebirds, including American Black Oystercatchers, Black and Ruddy Turnstones, Wandering Tattlers, Whimbrels, and Surfbirds. Look to the rockiest and most tide-washed portion of the reef for a Rock Sandpiper which is present nearly every winter. It is usually found in the company of Surfbirds. When the tide is high these shorebirds seek refuge on isolated jetties within the harbor and are often difficult to find. If your timing is perfect you can usually find these shorebirds—including the Rock Sandpiper—on the flat rocks inside the harbor just where the jetty begins in the northwest corner. Timing is critical. These rocks are covered at high tide and are productive only for the first half hour after the outgoing tide exposes them. Scan the sheer rock cliffs below the radar station for nesting Pelagic Cormorants, Belted Kingfishers, and Northern Rough-winged Swallows in Spring and Summer.

After you return to the parking lot, you may wish to take a short hike up the hill north of the radar station to a bluff above the beach. This can be a good vantage point for observing sea birds. Sooty Shearwaters may be seen by the thousands in summer and early fall, often quite close to shore. Northern Fulmars are regular during the winter months, and in some years Black-vented Shearwaters occur in fall and winter. A good spotting scope, cooperative weather conditions and patience are necessary to spot them. The grassy and scrub areas in the vicinity of Pillar Point have turned up a number of rare songbirds in recent years. Tropical Kingbirds, Palm Warblers and Clay-colored Sparrows occur in small numbers nearly every fall (October–December).

Other good access points to Princeton Harbor are as follows:

- **The Main Pier:** the best place for close-up studies of loons and grebes. May be extremely busy, but worth a brief investigation.

- **The Pillar Point Recreational Vehicle Parking Lot:** A good place to scope the inner jetties for roosting gulls, pelicans and shorebirds. From the jetty here you can scope a good portion of the harbor.

Birds to Look For

Year-round
Brown Pelican, Pelagic, Brandt's and Double-crested Cormorants, American Black Oystercatcher, Western Gull, Glaucous-winged Gull, Common Murre, Black Phoebe, Common Yellowthroat, White-crowned Sparrow (*nuttalli* race), Western Meadowlark, Belted Kingfisher.

Migrants
Brant, Snowy Plover, Spotted Sandpiper, Ruddy Turnstone, Baird's Sandpiper, Pectoral Sandpiper, Red-necked Phalarope, Red Phalarope, Parasitic Jaeger, Bonaparte's Gull, Black-legged Kittiwake (rare).

Summer Visitors
Sooty Shearwater, Heermann's Gull, Caspian Tern, Elegant Tern, Pigeon Guillemot, Northern Rough-winged Swallow, Barn Swallow, Yellow Warbler.

Winter Visitors
Red-throated, Common and Pacific Loons, Eared, Horned, Pied-billed, Western, Clark's and Red-necked (rare) Grebes, Northern Fulmar, Black-crowned Night Heron, Oldsquaw (rare), White-winged, Black and Surf Scoters, Red-breasted Merganser, Peregrine Falcon (rare), Virginia Rail, Sora, Wandering Tattler, Whimbrel, Black Turnstone, Surfbird, Rock Sandpiper (rare), Mew Gull, Marbled Murrelet, Ancient Murrelet, Glaucous Gull (rare), Say's Phoebe, Marsh Wren, Lincoln's Sparrow, Savannah Sparrow, Tricolored Blackbird.

Directions

The harbor is located just west of Coast Highway One, 18 miles south of San Francisco and 4 miles north of Half Moon Bay.

Facilities

Restrooms are available at the public parking areas. Restaurants, fish markets, convenience stores and a few hotels are in the harbor area.

Other Nearby Points of Interest

Fitzgerald Marine Refuge is located just north of Princeton Harbor in Moss Beach (a sign on the highway will point the way). This is a multiple-use area known to scientists as an incredibly rich intertidal region. Its tide pools are famous. Twenty-five previously unknown invertebrate species were discovered here. Three endemic invertebrate species and 49 species at the extreme southern limit of their range contribute to the unique nature of the habitat. The reserve is a county park and is open to the public. Shorebirds typical of rocky shorelines occur here at low tide. It is also a good place to scope for seabirds. The cypress groves above the beach and the willows along Lake Road south of the parking lot are locally famous spots for finding "vagrant" songbirds during Fall migration. Thirty warbler species have been recorded from here.

    Pilarcitos Creek Mouth lies between Half Moon Bay and Princeton Harbor. Access is by walking south from the parking lot at Venice Beach or by walking north from the parking lot at Half Moon Bay State Beach. (This parking lot is at the seaward end of Kelly Street in Half Moon Bay. If you're heading south, take a right onto Kelly Street at the third set of traffic signals in Half Moon Bay and the last right off Kelly Street to Half Moon Bay State Beach.) Fees are required at either of these parking lots. This is an extensive sandy beach with gently rolling dunes. Usually a few Snowy Plovers may be found in the area. In the summer, watch out for and keep out of any posted nesting areas of this critically threatened species. This beach, and especially the creek mouth, are known as a major gull roosting site. It can be a good place to pick Thayer's Gull out from among the Herring Gulls. A Glaucous Gull occasionally shows up here in winter. If Pilarcitos Creek is flowing to the sea, check the willows and scrubby growth nearby.

PESCADERO MARSH

❖

Peter J. Metropulos and Cliff Richer
Updated by Peter J. Metropulos

Spring ★★★★
Summer ★★
Fall ★★★★ (Best)
Winter ★★★★

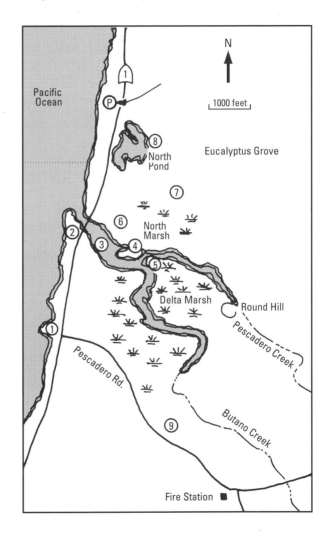

If San Mateo County birders had to name a single favorite San Francisco Peninsula locality, many would choose Pescadero. This location, on our scenic south coast, embraces a variety of habitats from rocky shoreline and sand dunes to freshwater marsh, coastal scrub, riparian woodland, grassland and croplands. Many excellent birding spots can be found within a short distance, and services (food, gas, etc.) are readily available.

Pescadero Marsh, situated directly on the Pacific Flyway, serves as an important stop-over point for migrant shorebirds, a wintering ground for numerous waterfowl, and a breeding ground for a variety of marsh birds. As the only sizable marsh on the California coast between San Francisco Bay and Monterey County it is a rare and valuable resource. A rich and diverse combination of habitats occurs here and visitors will enjoy excellent birding at all seasons.

Resident birds, breeding in the marsh, include Pied-billed Grebes, Great Blue Herons, Mallards, Cinnamon Teals, Gadwalls, Ruddy Ducks, American Coots, Virginia Rails, White-tailed Kites, Northern Harriers, Black Phoebes, Marsh Wrens, Common Yellowthroats, and Savannah and Song Sparrows. In winter, a few hundred ducks congregate in the marsh. The majority are dabblers but there are also a small number of diving ducks, such as goldeneyes, Buffleheads, scaup, Canvasbacks, and Ring-necked Ducks. A Eurasian Wigeon occasionally winters here. Some of the more uncommon raptors such as Golden Eagle, Osprey, Merlin and Peregrine Falcon are observed here each fall and winter. Regular winter residents include Great and Snowy Egrets, Black-crowned Night-Herons, Soras, Say's Phoebes, American Pipits, Common Snipe and Lincoln's Sparrows. Rare elsewhere in our area in winter, swallows may often be found in the marsh, mainly Violet-green and Tree Swallows (Tree Swallows nest here as well). A few White-throated Swifts are usually present with the wintering swallows.

Fall migration is the season when unusual migrant shorebirds are apt to be found. From early August through October, a keen observer could tally 30 or more species of shorebirds at Pescadero Marsh and the adjoining beach. Of course, the number of these birds present will depend upon availability of mudflats. Conditions are best when ponds and the estuary are shallow and large portions of mudflat are exposed. In fall, virtually any shorebird in western North America could show up here, and extreme rarities have been recorded (Bar-tailed Godwit, Ruff, Curlew Sandpiper, Stilt Sandpiper, Sharp-tailed Sandpiper). Species considered rare in our area but which are regular and to be expected in small numbers at Pescadero Marsh each fall are Pacific Golden-Plover and American Golden-Plover (from August–October), Lesser Yellowlegs (August–October), Solitary Sandpipers (September), Semipalmated Sandpipers (August–early September), Baird's Sandpipers (August–early October), Pectoral

Sandpipers (August–early November), Wilson's Phalaropes (July–September) and Red Phalaropes (late October–early December).

Pescadero Beach Parking Lots 1 and 2   Most birders prefer to park at one of these lots, bird the ocean and shoreline, then walk across the highway to Pescadero Marsh.

As you head south on Highway One, slow down as soon as you cross the concrete bridge over Pescadero Creek. You will soon thereafter make a sharp right turn into the parking area. Proceed north on this road through the parking lot until it ends at a bluff overlooking Pescadero Creek and Beach (**Parking lot #2**). This offers an overview of the marsh and creek estuary as well. With a scope you can scrutinize the terns, gulls and shorebirds below without exerting much effort. Examine the sandy expanses of beach below, looking for roosting gulls (Heermann's is common in summer and fall) and shorebirds typical of sandy beaches.

If you continue south a short distance you will arrive at the well-marked Pescadero Road intersection. **Parking lot # 1** is just west of this intersection. Set up your scope anywhere on the bluff above the beach and scan the rocks along the shore below. American Black Oystercatchers are almost always here. From late summer through spring look for Surfbird, Black and Ruddy Turnstone, Wandering Tattler and Whimbrel here. The rare Rock Sandpiper is also a possibility in winter, but is more likely at Pebble Beach, 2+ miles south of Pescadero. Scoters (all three species), loons, cormorants and murres may be present on the ocean, especially in winter. A few pairs of Marbled Murrelets are usually foraging a short distance beyond the surf, although calm waters and a spotting scope are often necessary to pick them out from shore. Likewise, a few Ancient Murrelets are present here in some years during winter. Further offshore, scan for Rhinoceros Auklets (year-round), Pigeon Guillemots (Spring and Summer) and shearwaters (year-round).

The Creek Mouth (#3)   The Sequoia Audubon Trail along the creek estuary begins on the east side of Highway One, below the north end of the bridge. The lagoon here has a relatively deep channel which attracts both fresh and saltwater diving birds. Belted Kingfishers and Northern Rough-winged Swallows often nest in holes on the cliff here. When conditions are suitable, shorebirds, gulls and terns may be present by the hundreds, but when water is high and the mud flats are not exposed, expect to see very few. Caspian and Forster's Terns are present in Spring and Fall. Elegant Terns are often conspicuous here from late July through October. They are highly vocal and easy to see. Baird's, Pectoral and Semipalmated Sandpipers, as well as Lesser Yellowlegs and Golden-Plovers are found here regularly during Fall migration.

The Confluence (#4) To your right, Butano and Pescadero Creeks join together before flowing into the lagoon. Generally, whenever two bodies of water come together, conditions favor those creatures that feed on the smaller aquatic life. Waders, dabblers, divers, and shorebirds may all be found here at times. At high tide when the mudflats are covered, this area can be quite productive. A family of Common Mergansers has been found here during recent nesting seasons. Proceed a short way up Pescadero Creek on the dike, checking the shoreline carefully. You may continue on this trail for ½ mile until the trail enters willow thickets and eucalyptus groves where a variety of land birds may be encountered. The trail winds up at an overlook on the hill to the east (watch out for Poison Oak in this area). Green Herons, Wood Ducks and Yellow Warblers nest along Pescadero Creek east of here. From anywhere on this dike trail one may look across to a grove of tall eucalyptus. There is an active nesting colony of Great Blue Herons here during spring and summer.

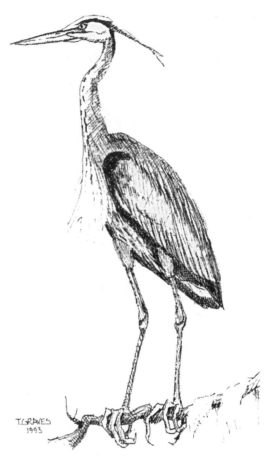

Great Blue Heron

The Spring (#5) Soon after you turn alongside the marsh, you will see a small pool on your left. This freshwater pool is apparently spring-fed and is a good spot for Common Yellowthroats. American Bitterns were once regular here but are now rare.

The North Marsh (#6) Return toward the highway along the top of the dike, stopping at likely vantage points to scope the marsh. If the water is shallow and mudflats are exposed, this spot is superb in fall for shorebirds. Although the smaller shorebirds may not be identifiable at this distance, you may be rewarded—especially in late fall—with views of Common Moorhen, Common Snipe, and even Virginia Rails feeding in the open. Black-crowned Night-herons, egrets, and dabbling ducks are usually identifiable as well. Diving ducks are present in winter when the water is deeper.

The Observation Point (#7)   North along the highway there was formerly a trail which crossed a small causeway between the marsh and North Pond. As of this writing, the only access to the former Observaton Point is from the North Pond trail (see below). Birding from the observation area itself is usually poor because of the distances involved and the angle of the sun, but it is a pleasant spot for a moment's respite from a hard day of birding. It is most worthwhile to check here in late afternoon when light conditions are optimum. Look down on North Marsh (preferably with a spotting scope) to examine waterfowl, herons, and shorebirds. Scan the skies above and below for hawks, including Rough-legged and Ferruginous in fall and winter, swallows, including Purple Martin and Bank Swallow as rare migrants, and swifts including Vaux's (uncommon) and Black (rare) during migration. If you linger long enough you may be treated to a spectacular sunset over Pescadero Beach.

The North Pond (#8)   The North Pond can be an unproductive area if the water level is too high, but always should be scanned, at least briefly. During late summer and fall if the water level drops enough to expose mudflats and small islands this pond can produce some interesting shorebirds. Various ducks, grebes and gulls often are on the pond as well. There is a parking lot across the highway from the Northwest corner of North Pond and a trail beginning at the northwest corner which nearly circles the pond. Occasionally you may wish to take this trail to get a better look at a shorebird feeding on the east shore of the pond, but it is not otherwise worth the effort. This parking lot is the main public access to Pescadero Beach and a fee is charged for its use.

South Marsh (#9)   Return to your car and drive south to Pescadero Road. Take a left and proceed 0.4 miles, where the road begins to run along the edge of Pescadero Marsh. The Butano Trail system which begins here at a dirt parking lot across the road from the highway maintenance station was severely truncated in 1993 when the marsh levees were breached to improve the flow of fresh water through the marsh . At this writing there are no plans for restoring this trail although there is considerable public sentiment to do so. You may want to check this location to determine its status. There are also turn-offs along the road where one can pull to the side of the road and look over the marsh and Butano Creek. Damage from years of siltation is obvious here and the growth of cattails is much denser than in years past. Visibility here is problem due to the thickness of marsh vegetation, but with luck one may catch a glimpse of one of the marsh's secretive denizens: Green Heron, American Bittern, Virginia Rail, and Common Moorhen are all resident. A Blue-winged Teal (rare, but regular) may flush up from the marsh in flocks of Cinnamon and Green-winged Teal. Scan perches in the open areas for resident White-tailed Kites and Northern Harriers. Barn Owls forage over the area in the evening through the year with an occasional Short-eared Owl appearing in winter.

Water Lane is a little used entrance to the marsh. If you proceed 1.1 miles from the marsh towards the town of Pescadero you will come to Water Lane on your left. Turn onto Water Lane and follow it beyond the pavement to its end. The buildings here are the Park headquarters, maintenance buildings and a ranger residence. Barn Owls roost in the trees above the buildings and in some of the buildings themselves. Two informal trails begin here. The trail to the left (as you face the buildings) follows the edge of the marsh and portions of it may be underwater at times. Rails seen along here tend to be trusting and very tolerant of human presence. Swamp Sparrows have been found along this trail in most winters. The trail to the right turns up the hill behind the buildings and parallels Pescadero Creek until it peters out beyond Round Hill. Wood Ducks and Green Herons can often be seen in the creek and seven species of swallows have been recorded from here in spring and early summer. In winter the grasslands here are feeding grounds for an astounding variety of sparrows and finches. Wood rat nests of considerable size can be found in the riparian growth.

The Future   The State of California has further plans to expand and restore the marsh. Currently (1996) these plans have resulted in the acquisition of neighboring farmland along Water Lane by long-term leases and outright purchase. These lands have been removed from cultivation and will be allowed to revert to marshland and open fields. Another proposed acquisition along the coast - if completed - will be re-vegetated to help control erosion and siltation of the marsh. Some of the existing levees are being breached, culverted or reduced in height so as to allow the water to resume more natural flow and (it is hoped) clear much of the loose silt from the marsh. All of these changes are intended to restore the marsh to a more natural condition and enhance the habitat. The changes to the Butano Trail have been referred to above. Other changes in the trail system are likely before the restoration is complete.

Directions

From anywhere on the peninsula, take the Bayshore Freeway (Highway 101) or Interstate 280 to Highway 92. Take 92 west to Half Moon Bay and follow it to the end. Turn south (left) on the Coastal Highway (Route 1) and in approximately 15 miles you will see signs for Pescadero State Beach. The marsh is on the opposite side of the road from the beach. From San Francisco follow I-280 to its intersection with Highway 1 south of Daly City and follow Highway 1 down the coast.

Facilities

There are portable toilets at both of the south parking lots and at the northern parking lot for Pescadero Beach (across from North Pond). The nearby town of Pescadero has a gas station, restaurants and markets.

Fee

There is a parking fee at the northern Pescadero Beach parking lot.

Special Notes

If you are in a hurry or if you are just passing by, you should concentrate your attention on the areas that can be seen from the roads and parking lots. At low tide you should be able to see and identify (with the help of a good spotting scope) most of the expected ducks and waders from parking lot #2. You can no longer park on the highway while birding, but you can usually get away with a brief stop while you scan the North Pond from inside the car. The upper portions of the marsh can be checked from the pullouts on Pescadero Road. Regardless of season, dress in layers for changeable coastal weather. In spring and summer be on the alert for ticks.

Publications

Sequoia Audubon Society has published a Checklist of the Birds of Pescadero Marsh. Contact the chapter office for details.

PESCADERO

❖

Peter J. Metropulos

If you continue east past the marsh another mile on Pescadero Road, you will arrive at the quaint agricultural community of Pescadero. There are restaurants, stores and a gas station here in the town center at the intersection of Pescadero and Stage Roads. If you don't care for a "sit-down" meal you can get sandwiches and baked goods at the town's two grocery stores.

Pescadero Creek passes under the Stage Road bridge near the town's church ½ mile east of the town's stop light. You can park and walk down to the creek where willows and cottonwoods and a thick understory provide excellent habitat for songbirds. This stretch of riparian woodland running through town has proven productive for rare wintering and fall migrant warblers in recent years. The creek can be checked from a few other places along Pescadero Road heading east of town (such as behind Duarte's Tavern), but be sure to respect local property rights in this area.

If you follow Pescadero Road east from town you will cross a bridge and come upon a farm to your right. (One mile). A colorful sign along the road will identify this as Phipps Ranch. (See map on page 125.) Not only is this a charming location to spend an hour or two birding, it's also a great spot to bring children and non-birders. Park in front of the fruit-and-vegetable stand and stroll through the greenhouse, aviary and animal pens and along the creek. There are lots of birds here, both domestic and wild. (Sorry, you can't count the fancy caged ones on your "life list.") A path will lead you west along a willow-lined stream, past a pick-your-own berry patch and herb garden, and eventually to tall alders along Pescadero Creek. There is a delightful mixture of native and exotic vegetation along the stretch of creek bordering the ranch, and birds are usually abundant, especially in fall and winter when many vagrant warblers, vireos, sparrows and flycatchers have been identified. Check the roving flocks of bushtits and chickadees for the occasional "vagrant" songbird during this time of year. Scrutinize the many sparrow flocks along the edges of weedy fields. White-throated and Swamp Sparrows occur in small numbers each winter.

PIGEON POINT

❖

Peter J. Metropulos

Spring ★★★★ (Best)
Summer ★★★★
Fall ★★★★
Winter ★★★★

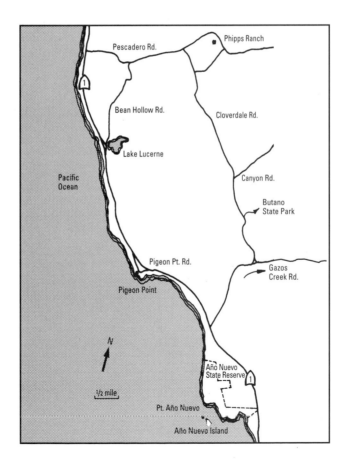

Located 50 miles south of San Francisco, Pigeon Point has become famous among birders as one of the finest vantage points for observing seabirds anywhere on the California coast. Its accessibility, geography (located immediately to the north of bird-rich Monterey Bay) and the presence of deep ocean waters very close to shore combine to produce excellent birding possibilities. Success can be extremely variable, ranging from fair to excellent, depending on season, visibility, observer's skill, duration of visit, and wind direction and velocity.

Park along the dirt shoulder of Pigeon Point Road anywhere north of the lighthouse facility. A good spotting scope is essential because on many days the birds are far offshore. By slowly and repeatedly scanning the sea from surf to horizon, a birder's patience is often rewarded. The best time of day for bird observation is morning when light conditions are most favorable. The prime time of the year is during spring migration (March–May) when thousands of north-bound loons, scoters, brant, cormorants, shearwaters, gulls, terns and shorebirds pass this promontory.

An intensive survey of migrant seabirds passing Pigeon Point in the spring of 1976 recorded over one million birds (most of them Pacific Loons)! To observe the numbers and variety of pelagic species here visibility must be good with no fog, haze or glare. A stiff breeze (10 miles per hour or more) from the West or Northwest is very helpful. When conditions are calm or wind blows from east or northeast, birding can be far less productive.

Check the tide-washed rocks below for the resident American Black Oystercatchers, as well as Wandering Tattlers (August–May), Surfbirds (September–April) and Black Turnstones (year-round). Pigeon Point is one of the most reliable locations, especially during spring and summer, for observing Marbled Murrelets. A few pairs are resident in the area and may often be found feeding just beyond the surf when the sea is not too rough. From November through February a few Ancient Murrelets are often seen here just offshore. During summer months feeding masses of Sooty Shearwaters are seen from here and may number in the tens of thousands.

In addition to seabirds, Pigeon Point can also be a good place to check for unusual land birds during periods of migration, especially Fall (September-November). Check the wires, scrub, and weedy edges of the roadside and Brussels sprout plantings for "field birds". Rarities such as Tropical Kingbird, Bobolink, Palm Warbler, Red-throated Pipit, Common Ground-Dove, and Clay-colored Sparrow have been spotted here. There are often a few Band-tailed Pigeons on the wires, especially in the morning. (Pigeon Point, however, was not named for its pigeons but rather in memory of the U.S.S. Pigeon, a ship that crashed into the rocks here early this century). Large flocks of Tricolored

Blackbirds may be found throughout the year in freshly plowed fields and cow pastures in this vicinity. Pigeon Point is also an excellent vantage point from which to scan for migrating Gray Whales during their northbound migration from March through May. Seals, sea lions, porpoises and sea otters are regularly spotted from Pigeon Point.

Birds to Look For

Common to uncommon species (to be expected in appropriate season):

- **Loons:** Loon migration in spring (March–May) can be quite impressive with rates of over one hundred birds per minute passing north not being unusual. The vast majority (over 90%) are Pacific Loons. The remainder are Common and Red-throated and by April the majority are in alternate ("breeding") plumage. All three species are found here virtually year round, a few even in mid-summer.
- **Northern Fulmar:** Erratic in numbers, but occurs in most years from November until March (a few seen daily); occasionally dozens in mid-winter.
- **Pink-footed Shearwater:** Uncommon to fairly common. Mid-April to October.
- **Buller's Shearwater:** Uncommon but regular, August to October.
- **Black-vented Shearwater:** Erratic in occurrence, being present by the hundreds some years; in other years they may be totally absent. Occurs October–March. Tends to forage closer to shore than other Shearwaters.
- **Sooty Shearwater:** Common to abundant, April–November; uncommon to rare at other seasons. Sometimes seen in large numbers close to shore.
- **Brant:** Fairly common in spring (March–May) when hundreds may be seen in a day.
- **Scoters:** Hundreds may be seen flying north in spring (March–May); over 90% are Surf Scoters, the rest are usually White-winged with an occasional Black. All 3 species may be seen here nearly year-round, a few even in mid summer.
- **Northern Harrier:** Resident in the vicinity. One or two seen daily hunting in open fields nearby.
- **American Black Oystercatcher:** Resident. A pair is usually present.
- **Wandering Tattler:** Uncommon, but regular, August–May.

- **Whimbrel:** One or two are usually present year-round; small flocks can be seen migrating north in April and May.
- **Surfbird:** Fairly common, September–April.
- **Red Phalarope:** Erratic; usually uncommon in spring (April–May) and fall (November–December). Stiff westerly breezes are usually responsible for their appearance. Hard to identify if too distant.
- **Pomarine Jaeger:** Uncommon April–May and July–October, with one or two seen on most days. Rare but regular in winter. This is the Jaeger most often seen here.
- **Parasitic Jaeger:** Uncommon April–May and July–October. Usually more regular in fall.
- **Bonaparte's Gull:** Common spring migrant (March–May), sometimes several hundred passing north in one day.
- **Heermann's Gull:** Common summer and fall visitor (June–November), uncommon to rare at other seasons.
- **Mew Gull:** Fairly common winter visitor (October–February).
- **Black-legged Kittiwake:** Erratic in occurrence. In some years it is very rarely seen, while in other years dozens can be seen in a day. Occurs November-May. A few normally present in winter, but often far offshore.
- **Elegant Tern:** Fairly common July–November. Numbers variable annually.
- **Common Murre:** Common most of the year (especially winter and spring) with a few often fairly close to shore. Thousands have been seen flying past Pigeon Point on some days in winter.
- **Pigeon Guillemot:** Fairly common spring and summer visitor (March–September), rare at other seasons. A few pairs nest on sea cliffs in the area.
- **Marbled Murrelet:** Fairly common to uncommon resident. A pair or two are usually present throughout the year, often fairly close to shore. Large numbers occur in spring and fall when over a hundred have passed Pigeon Point in a day.
- **Ancient Murrelet:** Erratic; usually uncommon winter visitor (November–February), often fairly close to shore. Not present each year.
- **Cassin's Auklet:** Quite uncommon, occurring further offshore than the other alcids. Most likely here in winter. However, most reports are of mis-identified Marbled Murrelets which appear all dark at a distance in alternate plumage.

- **Rhinoceros Auklet:** Uncommon to fairly common throughout the year. Most often seen in winter when hundreds have been seen in a day. Rare but regular in spring and summer when foraging birds from the nearby Año Nuevo Island colony may occur.

Rare to very rare species which have occurred here irregularly in small numbers, but are to be looked for:

- **Red-necked Grebe:** (December–April)
- **Black-footed Albatross:** Perhaps regular in very small numbers. (April–June)
- **Laysan Albatross:** A few records in March and April.
- **Short-tailed Shearwater:** Difficult to identify at a distance, perhaps rare but regular here November-March.
- **Franklin's Gull:** Several records in April and May.
- **Little Gull:** Very few records, all in April.
- **Glaucous Gull:** Several records. (December–April)
- **Sabine's Gull:** Rare and irregular but sometimes seen in small numbers in May.
- **Tufted Puffin:** Rare. (April–June)

Directions

Take Coast Highway One to Pigeon Point Road (just look for the picturesque lighthouse) about 6 miles south of Pescadero Beach. Park along the dirt shoulder of the road anywhere north of the lighthouse facility.

Facilities

No public restroom or water is available, but there is a public telephone. Public restrooms can be found a few miles north at Bean Hollow State Beach and south at the Gazos Creek Beach Access, both on Highway One. Inexpensive overnight accommodations are available at the Pigeon Point Hostel operated by American Youth Hostel. Call 415-879-0633 for information. The nearest food and gas are in Pescadero.

Special Notes

A good spotting scope and sturdy tripod are essential for good views. Dress warmly and be patient. Consult local weather forecast before your visit to get current conditions.

GAZOS CREEK AND CLOVERDALE ROAD

❖

Peter J. Metropulos

GAZOS CREEK

Spring ★★★★

Summer ★★

Fall ★★★

Winter ★★★

CLOVERDALE ROAD

Spring ★★

Summer ★★

Fall ★★

Winter ★★★

Gazos Creek Road allows birders access to a 10 mile stretch of forested coastal canyon, beginning at the sea and winding up the western slope of the Santa Cruz Mountains. Cloverdale Road begins 1.8 miles inland on Gazos Creek Road and runs north toward Pescadero through 6 miles of open, hilly grassland. Since most of the lands surrounding these roads is privately-owned, birding is restricted to the roadside (except at Butano State Park).

Gazos Creek Road begins on the east side of Coast Highway One about nine miles south of Pescadero Beach directly opposite the "Gazos Creek Beach Coastal Access" sign. Be sure to scan the beach here for roosting gulls and shorebirds and the dunes to the south for White-tailed Kites and Northern Harriers. Scope the calm waters just beyond the surf for scoters and alcids. You can find swallows foraging over the small marsh and Common Yellowthroats and Yellow Warblers are usually present in the willows here. There is a restroom at this parking lot. You should take advantage of it as there are no others nearby.

After checking the beach, drive inland up Gazos Creek Road, stopping at any of several dirt pull-outs along the road. The first two miles of the road are the most productive for birding. Here you will find yourself entering a cool, moist coastal canyon with hillsides of thick scrub and patches of Douglas Fir and live oaks. The shallow, rocky, year-round creek is bordered by a dense riparian woodland of alder, willow and elderberry. A wide variety of ferns, berry vines and flowering shrubs occupy the woodland understory and Spanish moss hangs from oak limbs above, creating a peaceful and luxuriant setting for a day afield. During sunny (and even foggy) summer weekends a moderate amount of traffic may put a damper on pleasurable walking on the road, but in early mornings, weekdays or off-season months, a short hike here can be quite rewarding. Not only will you find birds, but also wildflowers and other forms of wildlife.

Birding is best during the breeding season (March–July) when birds are on territory in full song. Expect to find a thorough representation of typical coastal woodland species. Walking along the road is the best bird-finding strategy, since birds are most conspicuous along the forest edge.

Gazos Creek Road will come to a junction 1.8 miles inland with Cloverdale Road. Continue on Gazos Creek Road as it ascends gradually into the Santa Cruz Mountains. The canyon becomes steeper and narrower and the coniferous forest becomes deeper and darker. The bird life in these woods is not as varied or as abundant as below, but there is a possibility of some of the rarer deep forest birds here (there are sightings of both Pileated Woodpecker and Spotted Owl). American Dippers nest in some years along the turbulent, rocky stretches of the creek and Hermit Warblers and Hermit Thrushes nest on the higher ridges. Note that the portion of Gazos Creek Road beyond the Villa Cathay Camp (5.3 miles from the beginning of the road) is unpaved dirt and may be closed when road conditions are less than ideal.

Owling anywhere and during any season along Gazos Creek Road can be excellent. Great Horned Owls and Northern Pygmy-Owls are resident in mixed woodlands, Western Screech-Owls in oaks, Northern Saw-whet Owls in deep coniferous forests, and Common Barn-Owls in grassy clearings.

The lower portions of Gazos Creek Road have become legendary in recent years as a prime location for discovering "vagrant" songbirds from eastern North America during spring migration. During late May through early July a dazzling list of eastern species has been recorded. Yellow-throated Vireo and Indigo Bunting, Hooded , Bay-breasted and Yellow-throated Warblers have been recorded and one or two Northern Parulas are found virtually each year. A pair even stayed to nest in 1990 for one of California's few breeding records. Similarly out-of-range, a pair of Rose-breasted Grosbeaks succeeded in nesting here as well during the 1980's.

Birds to look for

Year-round residents
Western Screech-Owl, Great Horned Owl, Northern Saw-whet Owl, Northern Pygmy-Owl, Anna's Hummingbird, Band-tailed Pigeon, Belted Kingfisher, Acorn, Downy and Hairy Woodpeckers, California Quail, Cooper's Hawk, Black Phoebe, Pygmy Nuthatch, Brown Creeper, Winter Wren, Wrentit, Hutton's Vireo, Common Yellowthroat, Purple Finch, Pine Siskin.

Dan Keller

Northern Pygmy-Owl

Summer residents

Vaux's Swift (uncommon), Allen's Hummingbird, Olive-sided Flycatcher, Western Wood-Pewee, Pacific-slope Flycatcher, Violet-green Swallow, Northern Rough-winged Swallow, Swainson's Thrush, Warbling Vireo, Orange-crowned, Wilson's and Yellow Warblers, MacGillivray's Warbler (uncommon), Black-headed Grosbeak.

Winter residents

Red-breasted Sapsucker, Say's Phoebe, Red-breasted Nuthatch, Golden-crowned Kinglet, Ruby-crowned Kinglet, Varied Thrush, Hermit Thrush, Townsend's Warbler, Red Crossbill (uncommon).

Cloverdale Road winds through rolling open rangeland with scrubby hillsides, willow-lined creeks and grassy pastures. After $2\frac{1}{4}$ miles (from the Gazos Creek Road intersection) you will see a sign marking the road to Butano State Park on your right. There is good birding along the entrance road ($\frac{1}{2}$ mile) between here and the first parking lot beyond the entrance kiosk, and plenty of possibilities for hiking within the park's extensive trail system. Butano Park is predominantly and thickly forested in Coast Redwoods and Douglas Fir with most of the same bird species as along Gazos Creek Road. A pair of Pileated Woodpeckers is resident in the park, although they are wide-ranging and not easy to see. Common Poorwills breed in chaparral in higher elevations here. Some of the species which occur as winter visitors to coastal lowlands breed in the higher portions of Butano State Park: Hermit Thrush, Golden-crowned Kinglet, Red-breasted Nuthatch and Yellow-rumped Warbler are among these.

One mile farther down Cloverdale Road brings you to **Canyon Road** on your right. Birding along this roadside (property here is private too) can be productive and worth a try if time permits.

Continue one more mile farther down Cloverdale Road to a gated dirt road on the left leading to the **Westland Nursery**. Walk or drive down this road. (Drive carefully. The speed bumps installed in '93 are vicious!) The small pond with marshy edges can be productive. The usual birds—coots, Ruddy Ducks, Mallards, Yellowthroats and Red-winged Blackbirds—nest here but there can be some unusual visitors in migration or in winter. Ring-necked Ducks, Soras, Common Moorhens, Common Snipe and Long-eared Owl have all been seen here. In addition to the usual grassland birds, the fields here are a favorite foraging spot for Great Blue Herons. A walk along the steep banks of Butano Creek can turn up a Green Heron or a pair of Wood Ducks. Keep in mind that this is a private driveway and you are there at the sufferance of the owners, so do not block the road. Park at the end ($\frac{1}{2}$ mile) or well off to the side and bird from the shoulders of the road. After checking the area, retrace your steps back to Cloverdale Road.

Pausing to look and listen at any of the dirt pull-outs along Cloverdale Road from April through July may produce a Grasshopper Sparrow singing from a wire fence or low shrub on a grassy hillside. They occur here in varying numbers annually, and are easiest to detect on calm mornings when their distinctive insect-like song can be heard often, in spring and early summer. Be cautioned that Savannah Sparrows breed in similar habitat here and also sing a high buzzy song. Grasshopper Sparrows can be looked for anywhere along the right (east) side of Cloverdale Road from Gazos Creek Road junction north for 5½ miles. They prefer gradually sloping hillsides with short grass and scattered coyote brush.

While you're slowly driving the road be on the lookout for large feeding flocks of blackbirds, particularly in the vicinity of grazing cattle. Tricolored Blackbirds are usually among them, often by the hundreds, from fall until spring. Sharp-eyed birders have turned up one or two Rusty Blackbirds in these flocks during some winters.

Continue on to the end of Cloverdale Road. At its end it intersects with Pescadero Road. A right turn will bring you to the Phipps Ranch (about ½ mile). A left turn will take you to the town of Pescadero (also ½ mile). Both of these areas have been covered in earlier chapters.

Other birds to look for along Cloverdale Road include raptors (Merlin, Peregrine, Ferruginous Hawk, Golden Eagle—all in fall and winter), Western Bluebird (resident), Western Meadowlark (resident), and Say's Phoebe (winter).

Facilities

There is a restroom at the Gazos Creek Beach Coastal Access and the park rangers at Butano State Park will usually waive the entrance fee for those needing to use the restrooms at the first parking lot. (*Please do not abuse this privilege as some of us value it quite highly.*) The gas station and restaurant at Gazos Creek Beach is rarely open for business so the nearest dependable food and gas are in Pescadero. Camping and picnic facilities available at Butano State Park.

AÑO NUEVO POINT

❖

Peter J. Metropulos

Spring ★★★★
Summer ★★★
Fall ★★★★
Winter ★★★★

Año Nuevo State Reserve is one of the most picturesque and ecologically rich areas along the central California coast. Located 55 miles south of San Francisco, the reserve boasts sweeping dunes, sheer cliffs, panoramic views of the Santa Cruz Mountains, an intricate plant community, luxuriant intertidal marine life, a major seal and sea lion rookery and a varied and unique bird community. The land that now encompasses the reserve has a long and colorful history, beginning with the sighting of Point Año Nuevo (Spanish for "New Year") by Spanish maritime explorer Sebastian Viscaino in 1603, and subsequently passing through several different owners' hands—mostly dairy ranchers and row-crop farmers. In prehistoric times it was occupied by Native Americans as a fishing and hunting camp. The reserve now includes some 4,000 acres of coastal mountains, dunes and beaches. The rocky 13 acre island is closed to the public to protect the thousands of marine birds and mammals which nest there. Año Nuevo has become famous in recent years as the most important pinniped (seal and sea lion) rookery and resting area in central and northern California. Hundreds of thousands of human visitors come each year to witness the spectacle of 3,000 or more northern elephant seals on their breeding grounds. During their December to March breeding season much of the reserve is closed and visitors can only tour the area on one of the regularly scheduled walks conducted by docents. **Advance reservations are usually necessary, particularly for weekends.** For advance reservations call Destinet at 1-800-444-7275. From April through November visitors must obtain a hiking permit to enter the ecologically sensitive areas. Current access information is available by calling (415) 879-0227. Birders can, however, hike the trails all the way out to the tour staging area (see map on page 125) without special permission at any time.

A birding trip any time of year is apt to bring rewards. A spotting scope is highly desirable to get close-up views of sea birds and marine mammals. Be prepared for cool, windy, foggy conditions, even in mid-summer. To fully cover the reserve area, a 3 mile round trip hike is necessary, beginning at the parking lot and heading west to Point Año Nuevo. Many people find this to be a fairly strenuous hike since it entails hiking up and down through loose sand dunes in some stretches.

Just east of the **main parking lot** is a lush wooded area where birders can look for typical western forest and scrubland birds (see list). Walk along the road here, or take the trail south from the Visitors' Center to the bridge over Año Nuevo Creek. Scan the ridges of the Santa Cruz Mountains to the east for migrant raptors and flocks of Band-tailed Pigeons and the skies above for swallows and swifts.

Before taking the trail out to the point, stop in at the Visitors' Center to look at a selection of brochures, gifts, books, and informative displays. Pick up a checklist here for a nominal charge. There is an excellent overlook of the entire beach and dune area from the Visitors' Center picnic area. With binoculars (or using the coin-operated telescope available) one can get views of Año Nuevo Island and its reefs and cliffs without the hike. Steller's Jays and White-crowned Sparrows (of the resident coastal *nuttalli* race) will visit your picnic table for tidbits.

The main trail leads from the **Parking Lot** west through grassland and coastal scrub toward Año Nuevo Point. Stay on the left trail where the trail forks at the shipwreck exhibit and proceed until you arrive at a freshwater pond. The pond attracts bathing gulls and foraging swallows, as well as small numbers of diving ducks and grebes. Check the openings along the tule-choked shore for rails, American Bittern and Common Yellowthroat. The marshy area here is home to the beautiful and endangered San Francisco Garter Snake. Scan the tops of pines and cypresses for roosting kites. Before the trail passes the pond and heads up the hill, look down at the sandy beach below for roosting gulls and shorebirds, and beyond the surf for grebes, loons, sea ducks and alcids. Descending to the beach you may scan the cliffs above to observe nesting Pelagic Cormorants, Pigeon Guillemots, Cliff Swallows, and Bank Swallows (all April–July). Marbled Murrelets are resident here and easiest to see from March–September when they are often seen in pairs just offshore. Amazing as it may seem, these small alcids build nests of moss on limbs of tall coniferous trees in the Santa Cruz Mountains a few miles inland from here.

Hiking out to the point from the pond area, keep a constant watch to the sky for foraging birds-of-prey: harriers, vultures, kestrels, Red-tailed Hawks and White-tailed Kites are all resident. During migration and winter other species are possible (Peregrine, Merlin, Osprey, Rough-legged Hawk).

Dan Keller

Loggerhead Shrike

About ¾ of a mile from the parking lot you will arrive at the **tour staging area** where people assemble before joining the docent-conducted walk. Access is limited from this point on. Restrooms are available here.

Once past the staging area the habitat abruptly changes from grass and scrub to expansive rolling sand dunes with scattered clumps of low willows. This habitat is one of the few remaining active dune fields on the California coast. There are colorful wildflowers in bloom nearly year-round in these dunes (peak in spring and summer), much to the delight of botanists and hummingbirds. Brush rabbits will hop out of your way at nearly every bend. California Thrashers may be heard singing year-round from the scrub here although they are unusual elsewhere along the immediate coast. Where opportunities exist to scan the sea below the bluffs, check for scoters, Red-breasted Mergansers, grebes, loons, murres and other alcids. The Harlequin Duck is a specialty of the area, a few occurring virtually year-round, usually in turbulent water in the vicinity of rocks. When not feeding just off the beach they may be resting on an offshore rock. Scan the skies above the cliffs for foraging Black Swifts which nest in sea-caves here during the summer.

When you arrive at **South Point** you will be directly opposite Año Nuevo Island. The island and surrounding waters are home to thousands of pinnipeds (elephant seals, harbor seals, California and Steller's sea lions) and a few sea otters as well. During the winter months if you use a scope to look over the island you will be treated to the spectacle of hundreds of marine mammals and thousands of roosting Brown Pelicans, gulls and cormorants. Species which breed on the rocky island include Pelagic and Brandt's Cormorants, Pigeon Guillemots, Black Oystercatchers, and Western Gulls. In 1994 and 1995 a pair of Heerman's Gulls nested on the island—one of very few breeding records for North America. Small numbers of Rhinoceros and Cassin's Auklets have colonized the island in recent years, nesting in burrows on sandy bluffs above the beach. The waters around the island may be "alive" with marine mammals and foraging birds: Heermann's Gulls and Elegant Terns are common in summer and fall, alcids (including a few Ancient Murrelets in winter), diving ducks, scoters, grebes (rarely Red-necked), Common Murres. Great white sharks patrol these waters and are sometimes seen in the channel separating the island and the point.

The rocky intertidal area between **South Point** and **North Point** (see map page 125) is a protected cove. There are usually piles of tide-cast seaweed along the shore. This is a superb area for close-up studies of shorebirds typical of rocky coasts (both turnstones, Surfbirds, Wandering Tattlers, American Black Oystercatchers and Whimbrels occur here virtually year-round). During fall migration (August–October) the rotting kelp and the flies it attracts are feeding sites for migrant shorebirds: Golden-Plovers, Baird's and Pectoral Sandpipers and Red Knots are regular in small numbers at this season. Extreme rarities such as Ruff, Curlew Sandpiper and Buff-breasted Sandpiper have been recorded here during fall as well. Brant may be foraging in the kelp beds too, along with a variety of gulls (Mew Gulls are common in winter) and song birds including American Pipit.

North Point has a sandy bluff which often harbors a Bank Swallow colony in summer. A few Northern Rough-winged Swallows are usually found in or near the colony. Scan any perches above the beach for both Black and Say's Phoebes and Belted Kingfisher.

Directions

From San Francisco, take I-280 south to the Coast Highway, (California Highway 1). From the bayside communities of San Mateo or Santa Clara counties take either Highway 101 or I-280 to Highway 92 and follow Highway 92 west to Highway 1. Año Nuevo is on Highway 1, 24 miles south of Half Moon Bay and 23 miles north of Santa Cruz. A sign on the west side of the highway just south of some ranch buildings and just north of the San Mateo county line on west side of highway points the way.

Fee

Separate fees are required both for parking and for the tour.

Facilities

Restrooms are available at the parking lot and tour staging area. Water is available at either the parking lot or Visitors' Center. Food, gas, etc. are available at Pescadero 11 miles north or Davenport 10 miles south.

Other Information

The Reserve is open from 8:00 A.M. to sunset. Current information on access to the Reserve is available by calling (415) 879-0227. We recommend that you call ahead, as the access rules and limits are made according to the need to protect the wildlife and can change at any time.

Advance reservations for December-March tours can be made as early as November by calling Destinet at 1-800-422-7275.

Publications

The Natural History of Año Nuevo by Le Boeuf and Kaza. This book and other publications, including checklists, are available at the Visitors' Center.

Birds to Look For

Resident Nesting Species
Brandt's and Pelagic Cormorants, American Bittern, White-tailed Kite, Northern Harrier, California Quail, American Black Oystercatcher, Western Gull, Rhinoceros Auklet, Band-tailed Pigeon, Belted Kingfisher, Hairy Woodpecker, Downy Woodpecker, Black Phoebe, Raven, Pygmy Nuthatch, Brown Creeper, Winter Wren, California Thrasher, Wrentit, Common Yellowthroat, White-crowned Sparrow, Savannah Sparrow, Western Meadowlark, Purple Finch, Pine Siskin.

Year-round Visitors
(found in every month but not breeding in the Reserve): Brown Pelican, Harlequin Duck, Common Murre, Marbled Murrelet, White-throated Swift, Tricolored Blackbird.

Summer Visitors
(April-September): Sooty Shearwater, Heermann's Gull, Elegant Tern, Pigeon Guillemot, Black Swift, Allen's Hummingbird, Olive-sided Flycatcher, Northern Rough-winged, Bank, Cliff and Barn Swallows, Swainson's Thrush, Wilson's Warbler.

Winter Visitors
(September-May): Loons (Red-throated, Pacific, Common), Grebes (all 6 species, including Red-necked [rare]). Scoters (all 3 species, including Black), Common Goldeneye, Bufflehead, Red-breasted Merganser, Peregrine, Merlin, Virginia Rail, Wandering Tattler, Whimbrel, Ruddy and Black Turnstones, Surfbird, Mew Gull, Black-legged Kittiwake (rare), Ancient Murrelet, Say's Phoebe, American Pipit, Townsend's Warbler, Red Crossbill (erratic). Some of these winter visitors may occasionally be found "vacationing" at Año Nuevo during the summer months. Among these lingerers may be Brant, loons, scoters, Red-breasted Mergansers, and various shorebirds and gulls.

Regular Migrants
Brant, Pacific and American Golden-Plovers, Red Knot, Baird's Sandpiper, Pectoral Sandpiper, Spotted Sandpiper, Red Phalarope, Parasitic Jaeger, Vaux's Swift, Palm Warbler (rare).

OTHER SAN MATEO COUNTY
BIRDING LOCATIONS

❖

Francis Toldi

San Mateo County has a multitude of small parks and semi-wild areas not otherwise covered in this book. Space limitations don't allow us to cover these areas fully, although you can enjoy a morning or even a full day's birding at any one of them. The birds you might see would vary depending on the habitat. A quick look at any of the specific locations in this book containing similar habitat should give you a good rough guide on what birds you can expect to see.

The most promising of these locations are:

Along the Coast

- Montara State Beach in Montara (heavily used most of the year).
- McNee State Park in Montara (accessible by foot from Montara Beach; steep trails through coastal scrub and willow riparian areas).
- Any of the San Mateo County Coastal Beaches including San Gregorio, Pebble Beach and Bean Hollow.
- Lake Lucerne (often has surprises) and Bean Hollow Road (good for raptors in winter), both off Highway 1 just south of Bean Hollow State Beach.

Along the Bay

- Oyster Point (rafts of ducks off the point in winter) in South San Francisco.
- Burlingame Bayfront south of the airport (close to the airport hotels; Grebes, ducks and shorebirds abound in winter).
- Bair Island, part of the San Francisco Bay National Wildlife Refuge (a first rate wetland with limited access; its breeding colonies have been severely impacted by red foxes) south of Redwood Shores.

In the Mid Peninsula

- San Bruno City Park (heavily used but can be good, especially in winter).
- Junipero Serra Park (great views, some good oak woodland, but not a lot of birds) in San Bruno.
- Mills Canyon (mixed woodland and grassland; good for common land birds) in Millbrae.
- Central Park (urban park with common land birds and a few roosting Barn Owls) in San Mateo.
- Waterdog Lake and Sheep Camp Trail (oak woodland, chaparral, grasslands and a small pond; a good selection of common land birds and an ocassional vagrant) in Belmont.
- Jasper Ridge Biological Preserve (Stanford University; private biological reserve, with limited access but outstanding habitat—see *Birding at the Bottom of the Bay* for details).

Golf courses can be good birding areas. Access rules vary greatly from one course to another. Check at the clubhouse for permission to enter and don't get in the way of the golfers.

Some of our residential areas afford excellent birding. When you're birding near houses please respect the privacy of the residents.

OTHER BAY AREA BIRDING SPOTS

❖

Anne Scanlan-Rohrer
Updated by Francis Toldi

There are several areas outside of the San Francisco Peninsula that are favorites with local birders. Visitors to the peninsula who have the time to visit any of these spots should make the effort to do so. All of these areas are visited annually or more often by local Audubon chapters. The interested reader can find detailed descriptions of these areas in Jean Richmond's *Birding Northern California,* and Westrich and Westrich's *Birder's Guide to Northern California.*

The Baylands Nature Preserve in Palo Alto, at the eastern end of Embarcadero Road off Highway 101, attracts great numbers of waterfowl and shorebirds every winter. Developed levee paths and boardwalks traverse the cordgrass and pickleweed marshland and can provide good looks at rails, including the endangered California Clapper Rail, Virginia Rail, Sora, and occasional glimpses of the furtive Black Rail. Other species found here include American Bittern, White-tailed Kite, Northern Harrier, Western Meadowlark, Common Yellowthroat, Marsh Wren, and sparrows—Song, Savannah, the rare but regular Sharp-tailed Sparrow, and the occasional Swamp Sparrow (the latter two in winter). The Lucy Evans Interpretive Center sponsors slide shows, nature walks, and offers interpretive literature. Call (415) 329-2506 for more information. The Palo Alto Flood Control Basin, Mountain View Forebay and Charleston Slough all lie immediately south of the Baylands and can offer outstanding birding. *Birding at the Bottom of the Bay* by the Santa Clara Valley Audubon Society (415-329-1811) describes these areas and others in detail.

The San Francisco Bay National Wildlife Refuge encompasses parts of San Mateo, Santa Clara and Alameda counties. The main public access is across the bay at the east end of the Dumbarton Bridge (Highway 84). There are a few trails at the west end of the bridge as well. The salt ponds and marshes draw large concentrations of shorebirds fall through spring—most noticeable are the Black-necked Stilts and American Avocets. White-tailed Kites are usually seen here, and the increasingly scarce Burrowing Owls may occasionally be found glaring from obvious perches. Waterfowl, gulls, terns, and swallows are present at various times of the year. The refuge's interpretive center is located here. (Call 415-792-3178 for information on hours open and scheduled nature walks.) This portion of the refuge is well-developed for birding and hiking with a variety of self-guided trails. The refuge is also accessible from a number of levees and the railroad tracks in Alviso in Santa Clara County. The refuge's educational center is located here, but is not normally open to the public unless school field trips, seminars or meetings are being held. You are however allowed to walk in past the gate to explore the trails and boardwalks beyond the center.

Coyote Hills Regional Park is not far from the refuge's interpretive center. One of the highlights of this park is a boardwalk leading through the heart of a freshwater marsh. Many species of dabbling ducks can be seen in the marsh ponds in winter, and it is a good place to search for American Bittern, rails, and Common Moorhen hiding in the reeds. The park's other habitats include bay shoreline, grassy hills, fields, and some tree cover. The park is noted for its owls. Several years ago the park hosted a pair of Great Horned Owls and their young, a Barn Owl, a Northern Saw-whet Owl, and a Long-eared Owl, all within sight of the park headquarters while Short-eared Owls worked the fields and marshes at dawn and dusk. From the Dumbarton Bridge, take Jarvis Avenue to Newark Boulevard northwest, then turn onto Patterson Ranch Road; the park is at the end of this road. The Coyote Hills Regional Park headquarters number is 415-471-4967.

Lake Merritt is the artificial lake in downtown Oakland, across the bay from San Francisco. It is only a short distance from Highways 17 and 580. This urban lake is crowded with water birds in the winter, including mergansers, dabbling and diving ducks, grebes, gulls, and cormorants, often at very close range. Rare but regularly seen here most winters are Barrow's Goldeneye, Oldsquaw, and Hooded Merganser. The islands in the lake are noted for roosting and nesting Snowy Egrets and Black-crowned Night-Herons. There are usually a few White Pelicans on the lake at all seasons. The park area around the lake holds a variety of land birds as well, and has drawn Tropical Kingbird and Summer Tanager as winter vagrants.

Bolinas Lagoon on Shoreline Highway (Coastal Route 1) near Stinson Beach in Marin County, one hour north of San Francisco, is a wonderful haven for shorebirds, dabbling and diving ducks, gulls, and other water birds. Winter brings teal, wigeons, scoters, and mergansers to the lagoon; flocks of Brant use the lagoon in migration and Ospreys fish the lagoon year-round.

Audubon Canyon Ranch, an old dairy ranch that is the site of a Great Blue Heron and Great Egret heronry from March through late June each year, is on Bolinas Lagoon. The herons and egrets nest in the flattened tops of redwoods and feed in the lagoon.

Besides the heronry, the ranch has several miles of hiking trails, a bookstore, a natural history museum and picnic grounds. The Audubon Canyon Ranch organization sponsors a docent program and educational seminars for adults and children. The organization also operates Bouverie Audubon Preserve in Sonoma County and Cypress Grove Preserve on Tomales Bay. The ranch is open weekends, 10 A.M. to 4 P.M., March 1 through July 4; call (415) 383-1644 for more information.

Audubon Canyon Ranch is not associated with the National Audubon Society but is jointly sponsored by the Golden Gate, Sequoia, Marin and Madrone Audubon Societies. It is entirely self-funded. No admission is charged but donations are appreciated.

The Point Reyes Bird Observatory (415-868-1221) headquarters is one canyon south of Audubon Canyon Ranch. Their Palomarin Field Station is on the Bolinas headlands just inside the southwest boundary of Point Reyes National Seashore. It can be found by following Route 1 to the north end of Bolinas Lagoon, making a sharp left turn onto Olema/Bolinas Road, and turning right onto Mesa road; stay on Mesa heading towards the ocean and you will eventually find the field station. Bird banding demonstrations are held here throughout the year. This station is the center for PRBO's land bird research program. Visitors are welcome at both facilities but do not expect a guided tour unless your visit coincides with a banding demonstration. These are working laboratories. Like Audubon Canyon Ranch they are self-funded and donations are appreciated.

If you continue north on Route 1 to the town of Olema and turn off onto Bear Valley road, you will come to the headquarters of the **Point Reyes National Seashore.** Within its 100 square miles, Point Reyes contains a diversity of habitats that deserve the birder's attention. Duxbury Reef, Palomarin, Pine Gulch Creek, Five Brooks Trailhead, White House Pool, Shields Salt Marsh, Limantour, Tomales Bay State Park, Abbott's Lagoon, and Pierce Point Road are all well-known areas. The outer point, in the general vicinity of the Point Reyes Lighthouse and nearby dairy farms, is well-known for rare migrants and vagrants in the late spring and fall. The spectacular list of unusual species is too great to repeat here.

Mines Road, on the outskirts of the town of Livermore in the East Bay, is one hour from either San Francisco or San Mateo. This country road winds its way towards Mount Hamilton and the Central Valley and is a favorite of area birders. Spring is the best time here; regular species include Phainopepla, Wild Turkey, Greater Roadrunner, Prairie Falcon and Lawrence's Goldfinch. The road branches at San Antonio Valley junction, where birders can continue over Mount Hamilton and back through San Jose, or turn east on Del Puerto Canyon Road to the Central Valley. Lewis' Woodpecker is usually found about 200 yards beyond the junction on San Antonio Valley Road. Del Puerto Canyon Road has areas where Yellow-breasted Chat and Costa's Hummingbird are regular nesters and

Cassin's Kingbird is occasional. The road continues on to Interstate 5 and back through Livermore. Both paths provide a good array of birds. This is a standard trip each year for the Golden Gate and Sequoia Audubon societies. It is best to go with a group the first time to discover the best birding spots along the road. Art Edwards of Mount Diablo Audubon has prepared a marvelous self-guided itinerary pinpointing all the birding stops and the birds you can expect to find there. You can get a copy by sending a self-addressed envelope to the attention of Cliff Richer at the Sequoia Audubon Society. Be sure to specify that you are writing for the Mines Road Itinerary.

The birding spots in the **Monterey Bay Area** are one to two and a half hours' drive south of the San Francisco Peninsula. One of the northernmost birding spots in this area is Jetty Road just north of the town of Moss Landing. The otherwise unimposing harbor, beach and adjacent small wetland of Moss Landing have produced an amazing number of rarities over the years. This may be due more to the number of birders passing by and the easy access to all of these from Jetty Road than anything else. If this is so it's a good argument for checking even the most unpromising spots.

Nearby Elkhorn Slough, a large coastal estuary near Moss Landing, is a bird "magnet" and undoubtedly contributes to the birding reputation of Moss Landing as a whole. The slough is a prime area to see wintering waterfowl and shorebirds. Several hundred of the slough's acres are managed by The Nature Conservancy. Information about Elkhorn Slough and TNC's other preserves can be obtained from their California Field Office, (415) 777-0487.

Monterey Bay and adjacent off shore areas attract a great number of pelagic birds due to its submarine canyon and the abundance of life in its waters. Debra Love Shearwater conducts boat trips on the bay on a year-round basis. Each trip is led by experienced birders and naturalists. Contact Shearwater Journeys at 408-637-8527 for more information. For the landlubber birder, the wharves and shoreline of Monterey Bay provide good looks at water birds.

Asilomar State Beach south of Monterey in Pacific Grove is a beautiful stretch of beach with tide pools and rocky shorelines. Cormorants gather in great numbers on large rock outcroppings here, and it is a good place to scope for grebes, loons, and scoters.

Carmel, a bit further south, is best known for its former mayor. But the two chief joys for birders here are the **Carmel River** and the various species found at the river mouth and upstream; and the **Point Lobos State Reserve,** with its large breeding colony of Brandt's Cormorants and the diverse mixture of birds found in its forests, meadows, and shoreline.

The **Los Banos Area Refuges** and **Panoche Valley** are usually combined into a weekend birding trip in February by the Sequoia, Golden Gate, and Santa Clara Valley Audubon Societies. As with Mines Road, it is preferable to go with a group the first time. **The Los Banos Wildlife Area, San Luis** and **Merced Wildlife Refuges** are southeast of the San Francisco Peninsula off Interstate 5, about two and a half hours' drive. The refuges attract thousands of geese and ducks, plus White-faced Ibis, Sandhill Crane, and raptors. A short drive south of Los Banos on Interstate 5 brings you to road J1 and the Little Panoche Detention Dam. This is the start of the route through **Panoche Valley.** Various stops along J1 can produce Mountain Bluebird, Lark and Vesper Sparrow, Rock Wren, Chukar (rare), Mountain Plover, Golden Eagle, Prairie Falcon, Greater Roadrunner, Lewis' Woodpecker, and Phainopepla. Birders return on Highway 25 through Hollister to Highway 101 through San Jose.

RESOURCES AND REFERENCES FOR THE BAY AREA BIRDWATCHER

❖

Fortunately for the eager naturalist, but unfortunately for the pocketbook, there are many fine references on birding and other nature subjects in the greater San Francisco Bay area. Restricting your focus only to birds would be a pity in this beautiful area. Here is a selected list of recommended further references and resources for your guidance.

Audubon Groups

Sequoia Audubon Society
30 W. 39th Avenue, #202
San Mateo, CA 94403-4561
(415) 345-3724

Golden Gate Audubon Society
2530 San Pablo Ave., Suite G
Berkeley, CA 94702
(510) 843-2222

Santa Clara Valley Audubon Society
22221 McClellan Road
Cupertino, CA 95014
(408) 252-3747

Audubon Canyon Ranch
4900 Shoreline Highway , Route 1
Stinson Beach, CA 94970
(415) 868-9244

National Audubon Society
Western Education Center
Richardson Bay Sanctuary
376 Greenwood Beach Road
Tiburon, CA 94920
(415) 388-2524

Bird Observatories

Coyote Creek Riparian Station
P.O. Box 1027
Alviso, CA 95002
(408) 262-9204

Golden Gate Raptor
Observatory
Building 201, Fort Mason
San Francisco, CA 94123
(415) 331-0730

Point Reyes Bird Observatory
4990 Shoreline Highway, Route 1
Stinson Beach, CA 94970
(415) 868-1221

San Francisco Bay
Bird Observatory
PO Box 247
Alviso, CA 95002
(408) 946-6548

Other Organizations

California Native Plant Society
3921 East Bayshore Road
Palo Alto, CA 94303
(415) 962-9876

The Sierra Club
San Francisco Bay Chapter
5237 College Avenue
Oakland, CA 94618
(510) 653-6127

The Nature Conservancy
California Regional Office
201 Mission Street
San Francisco, CA 94105
(415) 777-0487

The Sierra Club
Loma Prieta Chapter
3921 East Bayshore Road
Palo Alto, CA 94303
(415) 390-8411

Parks and Refuges

These addresses and telephone numbers are for regional headquarters. For specific parks, refer to the individual park listings in the local telephone directories, or call the numbers below for information.

California State Parks and Recreation Department
95 Kelly Avenue
Half Moon Bay, CA 94019
(415) 726-8820

Regional Open Space District
330 Distel Circle
Los Altos, CA 94022-1404
(415) 691-1200

San Francisco Bay National Wildlife Refuge
PO Box 524
Newark, CA 94560
(510) 792-0222

San Mateo County Parks and Recreation Department
590 Hamilton Street
Redwood City, CA 94063
(415) 363-4021

Western Region National Parks Information Line
Golden Gate National Recreation Area (GGNRA)
Fort Mason
San Francisco, CA 94123
(415) 556-0560

Transportation

Auto

For maps and road information call or visit the California State Automobile Association (AAA):

150 Van Ness Avenue
San Francisco, CA 94102
(415) 565-2711

455 Hickey Boulevard
Daly City, CA 94015
(415) 994-8400

1650 South Delaware
San Mateo, CA 94402
(415) 572-1160

20 El Camino Real
Redwood City, CA 94062
(415) 364-0620

For state-wide road conditions call:
Caltrans (California Department of Transportation)
Recorded Message 800-427-7623

Public Transportation

Bay Area Rapid Transit (BART) (415) 992-2278
San Francisco Municipal Railway (MUNI) (415) 673-6864
San Mateo County Transit (SAMTRANS) (800) 660-4287

Field Guides and Reference Books

American Ornithologists Union, *The A. O. U. Checklist of North American Birds* (6th Edition), Allen Press, Inc. 1983

Ehrlich, Paul R., David Dobkin and Darryl Wheye, *The Birder's Handbook,* Simon and Schuster, 1988.

Ehrlich, Paul R., David Dobkin and Darryl Wheye, *Birds in Jeopardy,* Stanford University Press, 1992

Farrand, John Jr., editor, *The Audubon Society Master Guide to Birding* (3 volumes), Alfred A. Knopf, 1983

Gilliam, Harold, *Weather of the San Francisco Bay Region,* University of California Press, 1962.

Grant, P. J., *Gulls: A Guide to Identification* (2nd Edition), Buteo Books, 1986

Harrison, Peter, Seabirds: *An Identification Guide* (Revised Edition), Houghton Mifflin, 1986

Haymon, Peter, John Marchant and Tony Prater, *Shorebirds: An Identification Guide,* Houghton Mifflin, 1986

Hedgpeth, Joel W., *Seashore Life of the San Francisco Bay Region,* University of California Press, 1962.

Hickman, James (editor), *The Jepson Manual: Higher Plants of California,* University of California Press, 1993.

Le Boeuf, Burney J. and Stephanie Kaza, *Año Nuevo Natural History,* The Boxwood Press, 1981

McCaskie, Guy, Paul de Benedictus, Richard Erickson and Joseph Morlan, *Birds of Northern California: An Annotated Field List* (2nd Edition), Golden Gate Audubon Society, 1979 with 1988 supplement

McClintock, Elizabeth, Paul Reeberg and Walter Knight, *A Flora of the San Bruno Mountains,* California Native Plant Society, 1990

Margolin, Malcolm, *The Ohlone Way,* Heyday Books, 1978

National Geographic Society, *Field Guide to the Birds of North America* (2nd Edition), National Geographic Society, 1987

Niehaus, Theodore and Charles L. Rippon, *A Field Guide to Pacific States Wildflowers,* Houghton Mifflin, 1976

Peattie, Donald Culrose, *A Natural History of Western Trees,* University of Nebraska Press, 1950

Peterson, Roger Tory, *A Field Guide to Western Birds* (3rd Edition), Houghton Mifflin, 1990

Petrides, George A. and Olivia, *A Field Guide to Western Trees,* Houghton Mifflin, 1992

Richmond, Jean, *Birding Northern California,* Mount Diablo Audubon Society, 1985

Rickets, Edward and Jack Calvin, *Between Pacific Tides* (5th Edition), Stanford University Press

Robbins, Chandler S., Bertel Bruun, Herbert S. Zim and Arthur Singer, *Birds of North America* (2nd Edition), Golden Press, 1983

Roberson, Don, *Monterey Birds,* Monterey Audubon Society, 1985

Rusmore, Jean and Francis Spangle, *Peninsula Trails* (2nd Edition), Wilderness Press, 1989

Sharsmith, Helen K., *Spring Wildflowers of the San Francisco Bay Region,* University of California Press, 1965

Shuford, W. David, *The Marin County Breeding Bird Atlas,* Bushtit Books, 1993.

Stallcup, Rich, *Ocean Birds of the Near Shore Pacific,* Point Reyes Bird Observatory, 1990

Stebbins, Robert C., *A Field Guide to Western Reptiles and Amphibians,* Houghton Mifflin, 1966

Wayburn, Peggy, *Adventuring in the San Francisco Bay Area,* Sierra Club, 1987

Westrich, LoLo and Jim, *Birders Guide to Northern California,* Gulf Publishing Co., 1991

Wyatt, Betty, Audrey Stoye and Cecily Harris, *Birding at the Bottom of the Bay* (2nd Edition), Santa Clara Audubon Society, 1990

Zimmer, Kevin J., *The Western Birdwatcher,* Prentice Hall, 1985

SPECIAL BIRDS AND WHERE TO FIND THEM

❖

Peter J. Metropulos

Species	Best Locations	Time of Year	Habitat	Comment
Loons (Pacific, Red-throated and Common) Grebes (Eared, Western, Clark's Pied-billed, Horned).	Fort Point (SF), Princeton Harbor, Año Nuevo State Reserve, Pescadero Beach, Coyote Point.	Mainly Sept.–Apr.	Harbors, bays, calm ocean waters	A few may occur during summer also. Red-necked is a rare winter visitor (one or two found each year).
Shearwaters	For close-up studies, join a deep sea sport-fishing trip from Pillar Point harbor; Using a spotting scope one can try for distant views from shore at the Cliff House in San Francisco and from Pigeon Point, Pillar Point, and Pescadero Beach;	Sooty: mainly Apr.–Nov. Pink-footed: Apr.–Oct. Buller's: Aug.–Oct. Black-vented: Sept.–Mar. Northern Fulmar: Nov.–Mar.	Open ocean	Sooties can be present by the thousands close to shore in summer and fall some years, rare but regular in winter. Black-vented is erratic in occurrence, some years present by hundreds quite close to shore, other years totally absent.
American Bittern	Pescadero Marsh, Sharp Park Golf Course (Laguna Salada), Año Nuevo State Reserve, Searsville Lake (off Portola Road).	Mainly winter; very rare and local in summer	Fresh or brackish marshes with cattails or tules	Has become increasingly scarce in recent years and no longer easy to find in Pescadero Marsh.
Green Heron	Lake Merced, (SF)., Searsville Lake (and adjoining marshes), Pescadero Creek.	Resident	Freshwater marsh and riparian woodland	Migrant and wandering birds apt to occur anywhere in suitable habitat.
Brant	Pigeon Point, Pillar Point, Año Nuevo State Reserve.	Mainly Mar.–May	Ocean waters	Hundreds seen moving north on some days offshore; stragglers may remain to spend summer or winter in harbors & bays.
Wood Duck	Searsville Lake, Pescadero Creek, Crystal Springs Reservoir.	Resident, but scarce and local in summer	Woodland ponds and streams	Frequents secluded locations, often ponds on private land. Usually shy, and hard to see.

Species	Best Locations	Time of Year	Habitat	Comment
Harlequin Duck	Año Nuevo State Reserve	Mainly Dec.–Apr.	Rocky shoreline with turbulent surf	Usually 1 or 2 are seen each winter. There are a few summer records. Migrant or wintering birds occur rarely, elsewhere along our rocky coast.
Barrow's Goldeneye	Foster City, Redwood Shores (Redwood City)	Dec.–Feb.	Saltwater ponds, lagoons, sloughs	Increasingly common in recent years; a dozen or two occur in winter, at each location.
Hooded Merganser	Foster City, Redwood Shores	Dec.–Feb.	Saltwater or freshwater ponds, lagoons and sloughs	A few also seen during winter at ponds and reservoirs throughout the Peninsula.
Black Scoter	Fort Funston and Ocean Beach in San Francisco; Pillar Point Harbor, Linda Mar Beach, Pescadero Beach in San Mateo County	Dec.–Apr.	Calm ocean waters, harbors	Small numbers occur anywhere along the coast; most common in northern portion; very rare on the Bay
Ring-necked Duck	Crystal Springs Reservoir, San Andreas Lake, Searsville Lake, Lake Merced	Oct.–Apr.	Freshwater lakes, reservoirs	Hundreds may occur in fall at southern end of Crystal Springs Reservoir.
Eurasian Wigeon	Foster City, Redwood Shores, Pescadero Marsh, Crystal Springs Reservoir	Dec.–Mar.	Fresh or saltwater sloughs, bays, reservoirs, marshes	Three or four occur in most years, always with flocks of American Wigeon.
White-tailed Kite	Año Nuevo State Reserve, baylands from Foster City south to Palo Alto, Pescadero Marsh.	Resident	Scarce and local during summer, Grasslands and open fields	Increasingly rare as a nesting bird. During other seasons apt to occur in suitable habitat anywhere south of San Francisco.
Bald Eagle	Crystal Springs Reservoir, San Andreas Lake	Nov.–Mar.	Freshwater Reservoirs	Typically a single bird will spend the winter in this area. Scan treetops or open ground along the shoreline for the bird.
Ferruginous Hawk	Higgins-Purisima Road, Stage Road, Cloverdale Road	Nov.–Dec.	Open rangeland, grasslands	Regular in very small numbers during late fall-early winter, mainly along coast from Half Moon Bay south.
Rough-legged Hawk	Half Moon Bay south	Nov.–Mar.	Open rangeland, grasslands, mainly in coastal lowlands	Highly erratic in occurrence. Normal winter will result in only 1 or 2, but during "invasion" years, dozens may be seen in a day.

Species	Best Locations	Time of Year	Habitat	Comment
Clapper Rail	Ravenswood Open Space Preserve	Resident	*Salicornia* saltmarsh with stands of cordgrass	Twenty years ago this bird could be found as far north as Millbrae. Now it breeds only from Redwood City south. The bulk of population is on Greco Island, San Francisco Bay National Wildlife Refuge, and inaccessible to the public.
Golden-Plovers	Pescadero Marsh, Año Nuevo State Reserve	Aug.–Mar.	Mudflats, freshly plowed fields, open rangeland	Pacific Golden-Plover is a fall migrant, but a few occasionally winter in coastal fields and rangeland. America Golden-Plover occurs only as a migrant.
Snowy Plover	Ocean Beach (best between Lincoln and Sloat) in San Francisco: Pilarcitos Creek mouth and nearby beaches, Linda Mar Beach in San Mateo County.	Mainly winter	Sandy beaches	Almost extirpated as a breeding bird on the Peninsula due to the increasing human usage of beaches and the recent population explosion of ravens, which prey on plover eggs and chicks.
Black Oyster-catcher	Seal Rocks in SF: Pedro Point, Pillar Point, Pescadero Beach, Pebble Beach, Año Nuevo State Reserve in San Mateo County.	Resident	Rocky shoreline	Very local during nesting season.
Wandering Tattler	Pillar Point, Pescadero Beach, Pebble Beach, Año Nuevo State Reserve	Aug.–May	Rocky shoreline	Widespread in small numbers along our coast; rare but regular inside Bay at Coyote Point.
Ruddy Turnstone	Año Nuevo State Reserve, Pillar Point, Coyote Point, Foster City shoreline, Pescadero Beach	July–Apr.	Sandy or muddy beaches	Prefer kelp-strewn beaches along coast; usually roosts at high tide with other shorebirds on bay.
Surfbird	Seal Rocks/Lands End in SF: Pillar Point, Pescadero Beach, Año Nuevo State Reserve in San Mateo County.	Aug.–May	Rocky shores	Check carefully among flocks of these birds for the rare Rock Sandpiper.
Red Knot	Foster City shoreline, Coyote Point	Aug.–Apr.	Gravelly or muddy shoreline; shellbars for roosting	Winter roosts of over 100 birds not unusual at Foster City.
Baird's Sandpiper	Pescadero Marsh, Año Nuevo State Reserve, Pillar Point marsh	Aug.–Sept.	Muddy edges of marsh and ponds; kelp strewn beaches	Small numbers occur each year (less than a dozen per day in season).

Species	Best Locations	Time of Year	Habitat	Comment
Pectoral Sandpiper	South end of Lake Merced in San Francisco; Pescadero Marsh, Año Nuevo State Reserve, Pillar Point marsh, coastal ranch ponds in San Mateo County.	Aug.–Sept.	Edges of marshes and ponds	Small numbers occur each year in season (less than a dozen per day).
Rock Sandpiper	Pillar Point, Pebble Beach (south of Pescadero).	Nov.–Mar.	Rocky, tide-washed coastline	Single individuals have wintered at Pillar Point reef and jetties almost annually for the last 25 years. Sometimes a second individual is found. Pebble Beach is not as reliable as formerly. Check carefully among flocks of Surfbirds for this rarity.
Parasitic Jaeger	Seal Rocks and Land's End in San Francisco: Pigeon Point, Pillar Point, Pescadero Beach, in San Mateo County.	Aug.–Sept.	Open ocean; regularly entering harbors, bays, estuaries	Often seen at this season chasing terns or gulls close to shore, sometimes inside Pillar Point harbor, and occasionally inside SF Bay. Also occurs as a spring migrant further offshore.
Thayer's Gull	Lake Merced in San Francisco: Pilarcitos Creek mouth, San Gregorio Beach, Gazos Creek mouth, in San Mateo County.	Nov.–Apr.	Sandy beaches for roosting	Check feeding concentrations of gulls and roosts carefully during winter. Usually occurs where there are Herring Gulls. Small numbers occur each year.
Glaucous Gull	Pillar Point Harbor, Pilarcitos Creek mouth	Nov.–Mar.	Roosts on sandy beaches and jetties	Each winter one or two are found at these locations.
Elegant Tern	Pillar Point, Pescadero Creek mouth, Coyote Point.	July–Oct.	Near-shore ocean waters; sandy beach for roosting	Often common and conspicuous along the length of our coast during summer, small numbers within San Francisco Bay as well.
Pigeon Guillemot	Land's End and Seal Rocks in San Francisco: Año Nuevo State Reserve, Pigeon Point, Pillar Point, Pedro Point, in San Mateo County.	Mar.–Sept.	Near-shore ocean waters; rocky sea cliffs for nesting	Easy to study at Año Nuevo during the nesting season (nests can often be observed).
Marbled Murrelet	Año Nuevo State Reserve, Pigeon Point, Pescadero Beach, Pillar Point.	Resident	Feeds on calm near-shore ocean waters; nests in old-growth conifer forest in the nearby Santa Cruz Mountains	Spotting scope necessary for satisfactory studies. Check calmer waters just beyond surf. Usually seen in pairs.
Ancient Murrelet	Pigeon Point, Pillar Point, Pescadero Beach.	Nov.–Mar.	Near-shore ocean waters	Not present every year, but when it does occur can be fairly common.

Species	Best Locations	Time of Year	Habitat	Comment
Rhinoceros Auklet	Pigeon Point, Año Nuevo State Reserve, Pescadero Beach, Pillar Point.	Resident, but scarce and local in nesting season	Open ocean; sometimes seen from shore	In recent years a colony has been established on Año Nuevo Island. Foraging birds may be seen between there and Pescadero Beach. During winter hundreds occur a mile or more off-shore.
Western Screech-Owl	Huddart County Park, Edgewood County Park, Wunderlich County Park.	Resident	Oak woodland	Fairly common resident of wooded areas, especially in the fog-free zone, east of Skyline.
Northern Pygmy-Owl	Gazos Creek Road, Butano State Park, Purisima Creek Redwoods County Park, Portola State Park, Huddart County Park.	Resident	Mixture of conifers, oaks and other trees	Fairly common resident of densely wooded portions of the Peninsula.
Spotted Owl	Butano State Park, Gazos Creek Road	Resident	Old-growth coniferous forest	Extremely rare and seldom observed. Perhaps only a single pair occurs in this area.
Northern Saw-whet Owl	Butano State Park, Gazos Creek Road, Purisima Creek Redwoods Park	Resident, but scarce and local in summer	Coniferous forest throughout Santa Cruz Mountains	Fairly common at certain densely-forested locations during winter.
Black Swift	Año Nuevo State Reserve	May–Sept.	Rocky sea cliffs and caves for nesting; foraging very high overhead, often miles away	A few pairs nest here each summer. Rare as a migrant elsewhere along coast.
Vaux's Swift	Portola State Park, Butano State Park, Pescadero Creek County Park	Apr.–Sept.	Open sky above coniferous forest	Extremely local nesting bird. Requires hollowed-out tall tree trunks for nest site. Occasionally in chimneys such as at Portola State Park Visitor Center. Sometimes fairly common during migration along coastal ridges.
Pileated Woodpecker	Portola State Park, Butano State Park, Pescadero Creek County Park	Resident	Old growth coniferous forest	Very rare in the Santa Cruz Mountains, perhaps only one or two pairs. They are elusive, wide-ranging, and more often heard than seen.
Bank Swallow	Lake Merced, Ocean Beach and Fort Funston in San Francisco: Año Nuevo State Reserve in San Mateo County.	Apr.–Aug.	Sandy bluffs above beach for nesting; freshwater ponds for foraging	Colonies exist at these two locations. Wandering individuals occur anywhere along the coast at this season.
American Dipper	Portola State Park, Memorial County Park, Pescadero Creek County Park, Butano State Park.	Resident	Rushing woodland streams	Only occurs in streams which flow strongly year-round. Obviously very local in summer.

Species	Best Locations	Time of Year	Habitat	Comment
Blue-gray Gnatcatcher	Edgewood County Park	Apr.–Aug.	Chaparral and oak woodland	Fairly common in some years in arid, fog-free zone, east of Santa Cruz Mountains from San Carlos south.
Black-throated Gray Warbler	Wunderlich County Park, Huddart County Park, Portola State Park	Apr.–Sept.	Mixture of oak woodland and coniferous forest	Fairly common in wooded parts of the Santa Cruz Mountains from Kings Mountain and Woodside south.
Hermit Warbler	Butano State Park, Portola State Park, Wunderlich County Park.	Apr.–Sept.	Coniferous forest	Locally fairly common in Santa Cruz Mountains from Woodside south, mainly above 1000 feet elevation.
MacGillivray's Warbler	Butano State Park, Gazos Creek Road, Higgins/ Purisima Creek Roads	Apr.–Aug.	Moist, spring-fed willow thickets	Local breeder in small numbers in coastal canyons (west slope of Santa Cruz Mountains) from El Granada south. Very difficult to observe, but its ringing song is distinctive.
Grasshopper Sparrow	Cloverdale and Stage Roads (Pescadero), lower San Gregorio Road (Highway 84), Higgins/Purisima Creek Roads (South of Half Moon Bay), and Skyline Boulevard (Highway 35) from Highway 84 south.	Apr.–Aug.	Grassy hillsides with small scattered shrubs	Erratic annually in abundance and distribution. Fairly common in some years. Difficult to obtain good views, but distinctive song is often heard in calm mornings during the nesting season.
Tricolored Blackbird	Cloverdale and Stage Roads (Pescadero), Redondo Beach Road and Verde Road (Half Moon Bay), Half Moon Bay Airport.	Resident, but very local in summer.	Pastures, ranch ponds, freshly-plowed fields	Widespread in coastal ranch lands from Moss Beach south. Erratic in numbers annually, and does not nest here every year. Numbers declining in recent years. Formerly present in thousands, now by the hundreds.
Hooded Oriole	Urban areas with introduced flowering trees and shrubs. Occurs in sunnier neighborhoods in San Francisco and throughout the Peninsula east of Santa Cruz Mountains. Check city parks and other public locations.	Apr.–Aug.	Ornamental plantings. Avoids native woodlands.	Common and widespread, but not always conspicuous. Requires Fan Palm for nesting. Look for these palms to find nesting birds.
Red Crossbill	Golden Gate Park, Lincoln Park, Lake Merced, (San Francisco). Almost anywhere on the Peninsula.	Resident, but infrequently seen in summer. Usually found in winter.	Coastal groves of Monterey Pines and Douglas Fir	Erratic in numbers and distribution each year. Some winters this bird occurs throughout the Peninsula, other years it is nearly absent.

A CHECKLIST OF THE BIRDS OF
SAN MATEO COUNTY, CALIFORNIA

❖

Compiled by Peter J. Metropulos for The Sequoia Audubon Society
January, 1996

Symbols used in this list are defined as follows:

Seasons

W	= Winter	mid-December through February
Sp	= Spring	March through early June
Su	= Summer	mid-June through July
F	= Fall	August through early December

Other Symbols

@ = Regular breeder. Species nests each year.

Δ = Irregular breeder. Few nesting records for the county. Nests infrequently.

(?) = Suspected breeder. Nesting confirmation lacking.

+ = Former breeder. No nesting records in recent years.

(Int) = Introduced species. Nesting species originally released from captivity.

C = Common to abundant in appropriate habitat. Always present, and in large numbers.

F = Fairly common. Always present, in moderate to small numbers.

U = Uncommon. Usually present and in small numbers.

R = Rare. Observed in very small numbers, and perhaps not in each year.

X = Extremely rare. Fewer than ten records of occurrence in season indicated.

L = Local. Species restricted to a small portion of the county, or to a few locations, during season indicated.

e = Erratic. Species may occur in substantially larger or smaller numbers than indicated during certain years.

"Accidental" = Species which have been recorded fewer than ten times ever in the county. (See pages 173–174).

"Extirpated" = Former breeding species not observed in the county in recent years. (See page 174).

(Horizontal lines separate each family of birds on the list.)

This checklist includes a total of 423 species recorded in San Mateo County and its offshore waters. Species names are in accordance with the American Ornithologists' Union (A.O.U.) checklist, 6th edition, as amended. Nesting evidence exists for 164 of these species

Common Name	Season				
	W	Sp	Su	F	
Red-throated Loon	F	F	R	F	. . .
Pacific Loon	F	C	U	F	. . .
Common Loon	F	F	R	F	. . .
Pied-billed Grebe @	F	F	U	F	. . .
Horned Grebe	F	F	X	F	. . .
Red-necked Grebe	R	R		R	. . .
Eared Grebe	F	F	X	F	. . .
Western Grebe	C	C	U	C	. . .
Clark's Grebe	F	F	R	F	. . .
Black-footed Albatross		U	U	R	. . .
Laysan Albatross		R			. . .
Northern Fulmar	Fe	Ue	X	Ue	. . .
Pink-footed Shearwater	X	F	F	F	. . .
Buller's Shearwater	X		R	F	. . .
Sooty Shearwater	R	C	C	C	. . .
Short-tailed Shearwater	R	R		R	. . .
Black-vented Shearwater	Re	Re	X	Re	. . .
Fork-tailed Storm-Petrel		R		R	. . .
Leach's Storm-Petrel		R	R	R	. . .
Ashy Storm-Petrel		X	U	U	. . .
Black Storm-Petrel			R	U	. . .

Common Name	Season			
	W	Sp	Su	F
American White Pelican	U	R	R	U	. . .
Brown Pelican	U	U	C	C	. . .
Double-crested Cormorant @	C	F	FL	C	. . .
Brandt's Cormorant @	C	C	FL	C	. . .
Pelagic Cormorant @	F	F	F	F	. . .
American Bittern @	R	R	RL	R	. . .
Great Blue Heron @	F	U	U	F	. . .
Great Egret @	F	U	UL	F	. . .
Snowy Egret @	F	F	FL	F	. . .
Cattle Egret	R	R		R	. . .
Green Heron @	R	R	RL	R	. . .
Black-crowned Night- Heron @	F	F	FL	F	. . .
Tundra Swan	R	X		X	. . .
Greater White-fronted Goose	R	X		X	. . .
Snow Goose	R	R	X	X	. . .
Ross' Goose	X	X	X	X	. . .
Brant	R	C	R	U	. . .
Canada Goose @	F	F	UL	F	. . .
Wood Duck @	U	U	RL	U	. . .
Green-winged Teal	F	F		F	. . .
Mallard @	C	F	F	C	. . .
Northern Pintail @	C	U	RL	C	. . .
Blue-winged Teal	R	R	X	R	. . .
Cinnamon Teal @	U	F	UL	F	. . .
Northern Shoveler Δ	F	U	RL	F	. . .
Gadwall @	F	U	UL	F	. . .
Eurasian Wigeon	R	X		R	. . .
American Wigeon	C	U	X	F	. . .
Canvasback	C	F	R	C	. . .
Redhead	R	R	X	R	. . .
Ring-necked Duck	F	U	X	F	. . .

Common Name	Season				
	W	Sp	Su	F	
Greater Scaup	C	C	R	C	. . .
Lesser Scaup △	C	C	R	C	. . .
Black Scoter	U	U	R	U	. . .
Surf Scoter	C	C	U	C	. . .
White-winged Scoter	F	F	R	F	. . .
Harlequin Duck	RL	RL	RL	RL	. . .
Oldsquaw	R	R	X	R	. . .
Common Goldeneye	F	F	X	F	. . .
Barrow's Goldeneye	UL	RL		RL	. . .
Bufflehead	C	F	X	F	. . .
Hooded Merganser	UL	RL		RL	. . .
Common Merganser △	R	R	XL	R	. . .
Red-breasted Merganser	F	F	R	F	. . .
Ruddy Duck @	C	F	UL	F	. . .
Turkey Vulture @	F	F	F	F	. . .
Osprey	R	R	X	R	. . .
White-tailed Kite @	U	R	RL	U	. . .
Bald Eagle +	RL	RL	XL	RL	. . .
Northern Harrier @	U	U	UL	U	. . .
Sharp-shinned Hawk @	U	U	RL	U	. . .
Cooper's Hawk @	U	U	U	U	. . .
Red-shouldered Hawk @	U	U	U	U	. . .
Broad-winged Hawk	X	X		R	. . .
Red-tailed Hawk @	F	F	F	F	. . .
Ferruginous Hawk	R	X		R	. . .
Rough-legged Hawk	Re	Re		Re	. . .
Golden Eagle +	R	R	R	R	. . .

Common Name	Season				
	W	Sp	Su	F	
American Kestrel @	F	F	F	F	. . .
Merlin	U	R		R	. . .
Peregrine Falcon Δ	R	R	R	R	. . .
Prairie Falcon	X	X		X	. . .
Ring-necked Pheasant @ (Int)	RL	RL	RL	RL	. . .
Wild Turkey Δ (Int)	RL	RL	RL	RL	. . .
California Quail @	C	C	C	C	. . .
Black Rail	X			X	. . .
Clapper Rail @	UL	UL	UL	UL	. . .
Virginia Rail @	F	F	U	F	. . .
Sora Δ	U	U	XL	U	. . .
Common Moorhen Δ	R	RL	RL	R	. . .
American Coot @	C	C	U	C	. . .
Black-bellied Plover	C	C	U	C	. . .
Pacific Golden-Plover	R	R	X	R	
American Golden-Plover				R	
Snowy Plover @	UL	RL	RL	UL	. . .
Semipalmated Plover	F	F	R	F	. . .
Killdeer @	C	F	F	C	. . .
American Black Oystercatcher @	UL	UL	UL	UL	. . .
Black-necked Stilt @	F	F	UL	F	. . .
American Avocet @	C	C	UL	C	. . .
Greater Yellowlegs	F	F	R	F	. . .
Lesser Yellowlegs	R	R	X	U	. . .
Solitary Sandpiper		X		X	. . .
Willet	C	C	U	C	. . .
Wandering Tattler	U	U	R	U	. . .

Common Name	Season				
	W	Sp	Su	F	
Spotted Sandpiper Δ	U	U	RL	U	...
Whimbrel	F	F	R	F	...
Long-billed Curlew	F	F	R	F	...
Marbled Godwit	C	C	U	C	...
Ruddy Turnstone	U	U	R	U	...
Black Turnstone	C	C	U	C	...
Surfbird	F	F	R	F	...
Red Knot	FL	FL	XL	FL	...
Sanderling	C	C	U	C	...
Semipalmated Sandpiper		X	X	R	...
Western Sandpiper	C	C	U	C	...
Least Sandpiper	C	C	U	C	...
Baird's Sandpiper		X	X	R	...
Pectoral Sandpiper		X	X	R	...
Rock Sandpiper	RL	RL		RL	...
Dunlin	C	C	X	C	...
Short-billed Dowitcher	C	C	R	C	...
Long-billed Dowitcher	C	C	R	C	...
Common Snipe	U	U		U	...
Wilson's Phalarope		X	R	U	...
Red-necked Phalarope		C	R	C	...
Red Phalarope	Ue	Ue	X	Ue	...
South Polar Skua		X	X	X	
Pomarine Jaeger	R	U	R	U	...
Parasitic Jaeger	X	U	R	U	...
Long-tailed Jaeger			X	R	...
Franklin's Gull	X	X	X	X	...
Bonaparte's Gull	F	C	R	F	...
Heermann's Gull Δ	R	R	C	C	...
Mew Gull	C	F		C	...

Common Name	Season				
	W	Sp	Su	F	
Ring-billed Gull	C	C	U	C	. . .
California Gull	C	C	F	C	. . .
Herring Gull	F	F	X	F	. . .
Thayer's Gull	U	U		U	. . .
Western Gull @	C	C	C	C	. . .
Glaucous-winged Gull	C	C	U	C	. . .
Glaucous Gull	R	R		X	. . .
Black-legged Kittiwake	Ue	Ue	Re	Ue	. . .
Sabine's Gull		Ue	Re	Re	. . .
Caspian Tern @	X	F	F	F	. . .
Elegant Tern	X	R	Ue	Fe	. . .
Common Tern		R	X	U	. . .
Arctic Tern		Ue	X	Ue	. . .
Forster's Tern @	F	C	F	C	. . .
Least Tern +		RL	RL	RL	. . .
Black Tern	X	X	X	X	. . .
Common Murre +	C	C	C	C	. . .
Pigeon Guillemot @	R	F	F	F	. . .
Marbled Murrelet @	U	F	UL	F	. . .
Xantus' Murrelet		X	X	R	. . .
Ancient Murrelet	Ue	Ue	X	Ue	. . .
Cassin's Auklet Δ	F	F	U	F	. . .
Rhinoceros Auklet Δ	F	F	U	F	. . .
Tufted Puffin (?)		R	R	R	. . .
Horned Puffin	X	R			. . .
Rock Dove @ (Int)	C	C	C	C	. . .
Band-tailed Pigeon @	F	F	F	F	. . .
Mourning Dove @	C	C	C	C	. . .
Common Barn-Owl @	U	U	U	U	. . .

Common Name	Season				
	W	Sp	Su	F	
Western Screech-Owl @	F	F	F	F	...
Great Horned Owl @	F	F	F	F	...
Northern Pygmy-Owl @	F	F	F	F	...
Burrowing Owl @	R	RL	RL	R	...
Long-eared Owl Δ	X	XL	XL	X	...
Short-eared Owl Δ	Re	Re	RL	Re	...
Northern Saw-whet Owl @	U	U	UL	U	...
Common Poorwill Δ	X	UL	UL	R	...
Black Swift @		R	RL	R	...
Vaux's Swift @	X	F	UL	U	...
White-throated Swift @	U	U	U	U	...
Anna's Hummingbird @	C	C	C	C	...
Rufous Hummingbird		F	U	F	...
Allen's Hummingbird @	F	C	C	U	...
Belted Kingfisher @	U	U	U	U	...
Lewis' Woodpecker	Re	Re		Re	...
Acorn Woodpecker @	F	F	F	F	...
Red-naped Sapsucker	R	X	X	R	...
Red-breasted Sapsucker Δ	U	U	XL	U	...
Nuttall's Woodpecker @	F	F	F	F	...
Downy Woodpecker @	F	F	F	F	...
Hairy Woodpecker @	F	F	F	F	...
Northern Flicker @	C	F	F	C	...
Pileated Woodpecker @	RL	RL	RL	RL	...
Olive-sided Flycatcher @		C	C	U	...
Western Wood-Pewee @		C	C	F	...
Willow Flycatcher		X		R	...
Hammond's Flycatcher	X	X		X	...
Pacific-Slope Flycatcher @	X	C	C	C	...
Black Phoebe @	F	F	F	F	...

Common Name	Season			
	W	Sp	Su	F
Say's Phoebe	F	U		F	. . .
Ash-throated Flycatcher @		F	F	U	. . .
Tropical Kingbird	X	X		R	. . .
Western Kingbird (?)		R	XL	R	. . .
Horned Lark @	U	UL	UL	U	. . .
Purple Martin Δ		R	RL	R	. . .
Tree Swallow @	U	F	F	F	. . .
Violet-green Swallow @	U	C	C	C	. . .
No. Rough-winged Swallow @	X	F	F	F	. . .
Bank Swallow @	X	FL	FL	U	. . .
Cliff Swallow @		C	C	F	. . .
Barn Swallow @	X	C	C	C	. . .
Steller's Jay @	C	C	C	C	. . .
Scrub Jay @	C	C	C	C	. . .
Yellow-billed Magpie +	X	X	X	X	. . .
American Crow @	F	F	FL	F	. . .
Common Raven @	F	F	F	F	. . .
Chestnut-backed Chickadee @	C	C	C	C	. . .
Plain Titmouse @	C	C	C	C	. . .
Bushtit @	C	C	C	C	. . .
Red-breasted Nuthatch @	Fe	Fe	U	Fe	. . .
White-breasted Nuthatch @	F	F	F	F	. . .
Pygmy Nuthatch @	C	C	C	C	. . .
Brown Creeper @	C	C	C	C	. . .
Rock Wren Δ	R	RL	RL	R	. . .
Bewick's Wren @	C	C	C	C	. . .
House Wren @	R	U	UL	U	. . .
Winter Wren @	F	F	F	F	. . .
Marsh Wren @	F	F	FL	F	. . .
American Dipper @	RL	RL	RL	RL	. . .

Common Name	Season				
	W	Sp	Su	F	
Golden-crowned Kinglet @	Fe	Fe	FL	Fe	. . .
Ruby-crowned Kinglet	C	C		C	. . .
Blue-gray Gnatcatcher @	R	U	UL	R	. . .
Western Bluebird @	U	U	U	U	. . .
Swainson's Thrush @		C	C	C	. . .
Hermit Thrush @	C	C	FL	C	. . .
American Robin @	C	C	C	C	. . .
Varied Thrush Δ	Ce	Ce	XL	Ce	. . .
Wrentit @	C	C	C	C	. . .
Northern Mockingbird @	C	C	C	C	. . .
California Thrasher @	C	C	C	C	. . .
American Pipit	C	C		C	. . .
Cedar Waxwing	C	C	X	C	. . .
Phainopepla		X	X	X	. . .
Loggerhead Shrike @	U	U	RL	U	. . .
European Starling @ (Int)	C	C	C	C	. . .
Solitary Vireo @	X	F	F	F	. . .
Hutton's Vireo @	C	C	C	C	. . .
Warbling Vireo @	X	C	C	C	. . .
Tennessee Warbler	X	X	X	R	. . .
Orange-crowned Warbler @	U	C	C	C	. . .
Nashville Warbler	R	R		R	. . .
Northern Parula Δ		X	R	X	. . .
Yellow Warbler @	X	F	F	C	. . .
Chestnut-sided Warbler		X	X	R	. . .
Magnolia Warbler		X	X	R	. . .
Yellow-rumped Warbler @	C	C	UL	C	. . .
Black-throated Gray Warbler @	R	F	F	F	. . .
Townsend's Warbler	C	C		C	. . .

Common Name	Season				
	W	Sp	Su	F	
Hermit Warbler @	R	F	FL	F	. . .
Prairie Warbler	X	X		R	. . .
Palm Warbler	R	X		R	. . .
Blackpoll Warbler		X		R	. . .
Black-and-white Warbler	R	X	X	R	. . .
American Redstart	X	X	X	R	. . .
Northern Waterthrush	X		X	R	. . .
MacGillivray's Warbler @	X	U	UL	U	. . .
Common Yellowthroat @	F	F	FL	F	. . .
Hooded Warbler		X	X	X	. . .
Wilson's Warbler @	X	C	C	C	. . .
Yellow-breasted Chat		R	X	X	. . .
Western Tanager @	X	F	UL	F	. . .
Rose-breasted Grosbeak Δ	X	X	R	X	. . .
Black-headed Grosbeak @	X	C	C	C	. . .
Lazuli Bunting @		F	F	U	. . .
Indigo Bunting Δ	X	X	X	X	. . .
Rufous-sided Towhee @	C	C	C	C	. . .
California Towhee @	C	C	C	C	. . .
Rufous-crowned Sparrow @	RL	RL	RL	RL	. . .
Chipping Sparrow @	X	F	F	U	. . .
Clay-colored Sparrow	X	X		R	. . .
Lark Sparrow @	R	UL	UL	U	. . .
Savannah Sparrow @	C	F	F	C	. . .
Grasshopper Sparrow @	X	F	F	R	. . .
Fox Sparrow	C	C		C	. . .
Song Sparrow @	C	C	C	C	. . .
Lincoln's Sparrow	F	F		F	. . .
Swamp Sparrow	R	X		R	. . .
White-throated Sparrow	R	R		R	. . .

Common Name	Season			
	W	Sp	Su	F
Golden-crowned Sparrow	C	C		C	...
White-crowned Sparrow @	C	C	C	C	...
Dark-eyed Junco @	C	C	C	C	...
Lapland Longspur	X	X		R	...
Bobolink		X	X	R	...
Redwinged Blackbird @	C	F	F	C	...
Tricolored Blackbird @	F	F	UL	F	...
Western Meadowlark @	C	F	F	C	...
Yellow-headed Blackbird	X	X	X	X	...
Brewer's Blackbird @	C	C	C	C	...
Brown-headed Cowbird @	U	C	C	F	...
Hooded Oriole @	X	F	F	U	...
Northern Oriole @	R	F	F	U	...
Purple Finch @	C	C	C	C	...
House Finch @	C	C	C	C	...
Red Crossbill △	Ue	Ue	Re	Ue	...
Pine Siskin @	C	F	F	C	...
Lesser Goldfinch @	C	C	C	C	...
Lawrence's Goldfinch △	X	Re	Re	X	...
American Goldfinch @	C	C	C	C	...
Evening Grosbeak	Re	Re	X	Re	...
House Sparrow @ (Int)	C	C	C	C	...

ACCIDENTALS

❖

Species recorded fewer than ten times in San Mateo County and offshore waters. (Season of occurrence in parentheses).

Yellow-billed Loon (W, Sp, Su), Mottled Petrel (Sp, F), Cook's Petrel (Sp), Murphy's Petrel (Sp), Stejneger's Petrel (F), Flesh-footed Shearwater (W, Sp, F), Wilson's Storm-Petrel (Su, F), Wedge-rumped Storm-Petrel (Su), Red-billed Tropicbird (Su), Red-tailed Tropicbird (F), Red-footed Booby (F), Anhinga (Sp), Magnificent Frigatebird (W, Sp, Su, F), Least Bittern (Sp, F), Little Blue Heron (Sp), Yellow-crowned Night-Heron (F), White-faced Ibis (Sp, F), Wood Stork (W), Emperor Goose (Sp), Tufted Duck (W, Sp), King Eider (W, Sp), Smew (W), Mississippi Kite (Sp), Northern Goshawk (W, F), Swainson's Hawk (W, Sp, F), Mountain Quail (Int.) (Sp, Su), Yellow Rail (W, Sp, F), Sandhill Crane (W, Sp, F), Mountain Plover (W, F), Bar-tailed Godwit (F), Sharp-tailed Sandpiper (Sp, F), Curlew Sandpiper (F), Stilt Sandpiper (F), Buff-breasted Sandpiper (F), Ruff (F), Little Gull (Sp), Common Black-headed Gull (W, Sp), Royal Tern (Sp, Su, F), Black Skimmer (Sp, Su), Craveri's Murrelet (F), Parakeet Auklet (W), Least Auklet (Su), White-winged Dove (F), Common Ground-Dove (W, Sp, F), Yellow-billed Cuckoo (F), Snowy Owl (W), Spotted Owl (W, Sp, F), Lesser Nighthawk (Sp), Common Nighthawk (Sp, F), Chuck-will's-widow (F), Chimney Swift (Su), Broad-billed Hummingbird (F), Costa's Hummingbird (F), Calliope Hummingbird (Sp), Yellow-bellied Sapsucker (W, Sp, F), Williamson's Sapsucker (W, F), Least Flycatcher (F), Dusky Flycatcher (Sp, F), Gray Flycatcher (Sp, F), Eastern Phoebe (F), Dusky-capped Flycatcher (F), Cassin's Kingbird (F), Eastern Kingbird (Su, F), Scissor-tailed Flycatcher (Su, F), Pinyon Jay (W), Clark's Nutcracker (W), Mountain Chickadee (F), Canyon Wren (W, Sp, Su, F), Mountain Bluebird (W, Sp, F), Townsend's Solitaire (W, F), Sage Thrasher (Sp, F), Brown Thrasher (Su, F), Red-throated Pipit (F), Bohemian Waxwing (F), Northern Shrike (W, F), Bell's Vireo (Sp), Yellow-throated Vireo (Sp), Philadelphia Vireo (F), Red-eyed Vireo (Sp, Su, F), Golden-winged Warbler (F), Virginia's Warbler (F), Lucy's Warbler (W, Sp, F), Cape May Warbler (F), Black-throated Blue Warbler (W, F), Black-throated Green Warbler (F), Blackburnian Warbler (F), Yellow-throated Warbler (F), Bay-breasted Warbler (Sp, F), Prothonotary Warbler (Sp, F), Worm-eating Warbler (W, F), Ovenbird (Sp, Su, F), Connecticut Warbler (F), Canada Warbler (F), Painted Redstart (F), Summer Tanager (W, F), Blue Grosbeak (Sp, F), Dickcissel (F), Green-tailed Towhee (F), American Tree Sparrow (W, Sp, F), Brewer's Sparrow (W, Sp, F), Black-chinned Sparrow (Sp), Vesper Sparrow (F),

Black-throated Sparrow (Sp, F), Sage Sparrow (Sp, F), Lark Bunting (Sp, F), Sharp-tailed Sparrow (W, F), Harris' Sparrow (W, Sp, F), Snow Bunting (F), Orchard Oriole (F), Rusty Blackbird (W, F), Great-tailed Grackle (W), Chestnut-collared Longspur (Sp, F), Rustic Bunting (F), Cassin's Finch (W, F).

EXTIRPATED

Species formerly nesting in the county,
but no records in many years. (Last recorded year in parentheses).
Fulvous Whistling-Duck (1920)
California Condor (1971)
Greater Roadrunner (1946)

To our Readers,

We hope you have found this updated revision of *San Francisco Peninsula Birdwatching* both informative and helpful. As members of the **Sequoia Audubon Society of San Mateo County**, we welcome your comments, helpful criticism, or questions regarding birds in our area.

The mission of the **Sequoia Audubon Society** is to participate actively in environmental education, conservation, and in the restoration, preservation, protection and enjoyment of our native natural resources with emphasis on birds and their habitats. To this end, we invite you, the reader, to financially assist us in our development of local educational programs by ordering additional copies of this guide, becoming a member of the Sequoia Audubon Society, or making a tax-deductible financial contribution using the form attached below.

Thank you,

SAS Publication Committee

We invite your membership in **National Audubon Society** and our **Sequoia Chapter**. To join, to make a tax-deductible donation, or to request additional copies of this book, please complete and mail this form with payment to **Sequoia Audubon Society**, 30 West 39th Avenue, Suite 202, San Mateo, CA 94403. For additional information, call the Sequoia Audubon Society at (415) 345-3724.

____	**National Audubon Society Membership**
	New members pay $20 and receive *Audubon Magazine* and our local newsletter *Sequoia Needles*. Checks should be payable to National Audubon Society.

____	*Sequoia Needles* **subscription only**
	$10 for nine (9) issues/year.

____	**Tax-deductible Donation** to help fund our chapter's mission.

____	I request ____ **additional copies** of *San Francisco Peninsula Birdwatching* guide @ $14.95/copy plus $3.30/copy tax, shipping and handling ($18.25/guide).

Name _____

Address _____

City _____ State _____ Zip _____

Telephone Number _____